The Four Temperaments

*

Also by Renee Baron

What Type Am I?

With Elizabeth Wagele

Are You My Type, Am I Yours?

The Enneagram Made Easy

The Four Temperaments

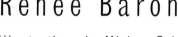

A Fun and Practical Guide to Understanding Yourself and the People in Your Life

Renee Baron

Illustrations by Miriam Fabbri

St. Martin's Griffin ✤ New York

www.stmartins.com

Illustrations copyright © 2004 by Miriam Fabbri

LIBRARY OF CONGRESS CATALOGING-IN-PUBLICATION DATA

Baron, Renee.
    The four temperaments : a fun and practical guide to understanding yourself and the people in your life / Renee Baron.—1st St. Martin's Griffin ed.
      p. cm.
    Includes bibliographical references (page 125).
    ISBN 0-312-31578-3
    EAN 978-0312-31578-8
     1. Four temperaments.   I. Title.

  BF698.3.B365 2004
  155.2'6—dc22

2003061181

First Edition: April 2004

10 9 8 7 6 5 4 3 2 1

To Rona Jackson, my late-in-life adopted mom,
for her unconditional love and support.

To Nancy Sabonya, my Diamond Heart teacher,
for guiding me toward greater self-love.

Contents

Acknowledgments

*

To my children, Jodi, Luna, and Dan, and to my granddaughter, Eliana. To Donna and Tom, my extended family.

To Ellen Odza, for a long and cherished friendship. To Sandra Delay, for the joy and depth of our connection. To Ellen Strong, my spiritual sister. To Janet Forman, Barbara Kaplan, Sharon Cohen, David Sapper, Janet Hastings, and Lois Brown, whose friendships I deeply value.

To Zoe Sexton, for her expert financial guidance and support.

To my agent, Shelley Roth, for her continuing support of my work and finding this book its home.

To Marian Lizzi, my editor, for her interest in this project and her astute editing of the final manuscript.

To Julie Mente for her assistance and support in bringing the book to fruition.

To Miriam Fabbri, for her wonderful artwork and the ease of our working relationship.

To the many people who gave so generously of their time editing chapters, especially to Beth Kuper, Cindy Wolley, Sandra Delay, and Margaret Miner.

Thanks to Naomi Lucks, Luna Baron, Ellen Odza, Janet Forman, Sharon Cohen, and Linda Petty, who gave feedback on a few of the chapters.

Knowing others is wisdom,
Knowing yourself is enlightenment.
—Lao-tzu

The Four
Temperaments

*

1 *

What Are Temperaments?

A happy life is one which is in accordance
with its own nature.
—MARCUS ANNAEUS SENECA

When I was growing up, my parents—like many parents—made the mistake of assuming that I was *the same* as they were. They tried hard to mold me into who they thought I should be. In order to gain their acceptance and approval, I tried hard to meet their expectations, but in the process, many of my natural strengths and abilities went unrecognized and remained undeveloped. When our natural abilities and talents have been undermined or overlooked instead of fostered and encouraged, every aspect of life is impacted, especially our self-esteem. As a young adult, I never quite felt like *myself*—and I wasn't even sure what "being myself" would feel like.

When I came upon a book titled *Please Understand Me* by David Keirsey and Marilyn Bates, I began to learn about personality temperaments, which are based in ancient traditions and informed by the ideas of Carl Jung and others. The moment I identified my own temperament, I felt a great sense of relief knowing there were other people like me in the world. After decades of trying to alter myself to please others, I came to realize that I was not defective, unworthy, bad, or wrong—in fact, I was perfectly okay being the way I was. My self-esteem began to flourish as I came to recognize and appreciate the value of my own unique qualities: being creative, idealistic, soul-searching, and sensitive.

This new perspective was so powerful and life-transforming for me that I felt compelled to share it with others. For the next twenty-five years I taught classes, led workshops, and counseled people using temperament and type to help them better understand, accept, and appreciate themselves. I encouraged them to use their strengths and abilities in careers that would be appropriate, rewarding, and meaningful. I also had the intention of helping people improve the quality of their relationships—by learning to be more accepting and compassionate of others, especially of those people who are different from them. I was particularly interested in reaching parents so that they could learn to understand and encourage their children to develop according to their own inborn natures and to support them in expressing and developing their authentic selves.

The Four Temperaments

According to temperament theory, we come into the world with one of four different inborn natures. *Temperament* can be described as a predisposition that is our true self. Since our temperament is inborn and not acquired, it can be observed from very early on. The seed is already there for a child to be an Ideal Seeker, a Knowledge Seeker, a Security Seeker, or an Experience Seeker, just as an acorn is primed to become an oak.

Temperament theory suggests that people of the same temperament share a fundamental need that is the motivating or driving force behind their behavior. Being aware of this need helps us identify what propels and inspires us and what will give us the greatest personal satisfaction. Because our core need is so much a part of our true nature, it is often invisible to us, and we often assume that everyone has this same need. Knowing our temperament also helps us to identify our core values. Becoming aware of these values helps us to understand what gives us sustenance and why certain things are important to us.

Our temperament also helps us to recognize our natural strengths and abilities, which can form the basis for our self-esteem. We often assume that others can easily do the same things we can, and we end up taking our gifts for granted. Our strengths and abilities are often better known to our friends and colleagues than to ourselves, for they notice the ease with which we do the same things that might be difficult for them.

Although we change in many ways throughout our life, our basic temperament remains the same. We may have skills from several of the temperaments, and access them when we need to, but one of the four temperaments is *where we feel the most at home*.

Which One Sounds Most Like You?

The four temperaments have been referred to by different names over the centuries (as you will see in the next section). Throughout this book, I will use the terms *Security Seeker, Experience Seeker, Knowledge Seeker,* and *Ideal Seeker*. Here are the basic characteristics of each.

Security Seekers are motivated by the need to be dependable and responsible in their social group (family, workplace, or community). They value the traditions, customs, and laws of society, which give them a sense of safety, stability, and belonging.

Experience Seekers are motivated by the need to act freely and spontaneously on their impulses in the moment, not just for fun, but for problem-solving as well. They live in the present, in the here and now. Experience Seekers value their freedom, action, and autonomy, and they seek excitement.

Knowledge Seekers are motivated by a need to constantly improve their base of knowledge and competency. They value the theoretical and the powers of the mind, and they strive to understand and explain the world around them.

Ideal Seekers are motivated by the need to be authentic, to understand their own and others' deepest feelings, and to discover what life is all about. They value using their insights and creativity to help themselves and others realize and develop their emotional and spiritual potential.

Although people of the same temperament have the same basic motivation and view the world in some fundamentally similar ways, there are several factors that account for variations within each of the temperaments. One factor is whether individuals are social and outgoing *(extroverted)* or re-served and reflective *(introverted)*. Another factor is whether they value anal-ysis and logic in making decisions *(thinkers)* or whether they prefer making decisions according to their personal or subjective values based on how other people will be affected *(feelers)*. You will read more about these dif-ferences in each of the temperament chapters that follow.

A Brief History of Temperament Theory

The idea that people fall into four basic temperaments is not new. Through-out the ages, philosophers, writers, psychologists, and other observers of human behavior have noticed four common patterns into which all people fit. In 340 B.C. Plato wrote of four temperament types, which he called Artisan, Guardian, Idealist, and Rational. In 325 B.C. Aristotle wrote of Hedonic, Proprietary, Ethical, and Dialectical temperaments. In 190 A.D. Galen spoke of Sanguine, Melancholic, Choleric, and Phlegmatic temperaments, which were based on the ideas of Hippocrates from as far back as 450 B.C. Paracelsus in 1550 A.D. wrote of Changeable, Industrious, Inspired, and Curious temperaments. The four astrological elements—earth, air, and water, and fire—are well known and have been described for centuries. Over the centuries this organizing principle, based on observation and theoretical speculation, has proved remarkably consistent, and it provides a basis for the use of temperament theory today.

In the early twentieth century, temperament theory was at first overshadowed by the revolutionary work of Sigmund Freud and Ivan Pavlov. While their theories were quite different from each other, both men saw people as fundamentally alike and sharing a single basic motivation for behavior. Freud saw behavior as driven by instinctual lust, while Pavlov saw responses to prior conditioning as the motivation for all behavior. Even though many of Freud's and Pavlov's followers came to disagree with them, most theorists retained the idea of a single motivation for behavior.

During this period, Carl Jung, the well-known Swiss physician, was among the few theorists of his time to view individuals in terms of patterns. In his book *Psychological Types,* Jung wrote about four groups of personality types based on their four mental functions—sensing and intuition, thinking and feeling. *Sensing and intuiting* refer to the two different ways we perceive or take in information: Sensing types focus on here-and-now reality. Intuiting types focus on the future, on possibilities. *Thinking and feeling* refer to the two different ways we elevate information and make decisions: Thinking types make objective or impersonal decisions based on logic and analysis. Feeling types make decisions according to their subjective values on what is important to them and others personally. According to Jung, these four functions are used in an introverted (inward) or extroverted (outward) way.

In the 1950s, Jung's ideas were given new life by Isabel Myers, a layman, along with her mother, Katharine Briggs. This mother-daughter team took the useful parts of Jung's theory and devised an inventory called the Myers-Briggs Type Indicator (MBTI) to help people understand and identify personality types and to appreciate people's differences. The MBTI is the most widely used psychological inventory in the world. It is based on Jung's four mental functions, plus extroverting and introverting, and includes the addition of Myers and Briggs judging and perceiving dimensions (how people prefer to live their outer lives). Judging types want to have things settled and decided as soon as possible. Perceiving types like to keep life open-ended. All the possible combinations of dimensions or preferences add up to sixteen different types. Myers describes the gifts of each of the sixteen types in her book, *Gifts Differing*.

In the 1950s, David Keirsey came across the work of Briggs and Myers, and in studying the relationships between the sixteen personality types and the four temperaments that had been described throughout the ages, he found a correlation between these types and the four temperaments of ancient thought.

The basis of Keirsey's theory is that the four temperaments (which he names Guardians, Artisans, Rationalists, and Idealists) are derived from two basic observable human behaviors: how we communicate (whether we are concrete or abstract in our use of words) and how we accomplish our goals (whether we are cooperative or utilitarian). Keirsey's theory is based on people's skilled actions, or their "intelligent roles," as he calls them. Each temperament shows its own intelligence is basically and fundamentally different from the others. In 1978 he published his bestselling book, *Please Understand Me*, which he coauthored with Marilyn Bates. It has sold millions of copies throughout the world.

This book builds on the theories of Jung, Myers and Briggs, and Keirsey. In the appendix I correlate these theories with another popular system of personality, the Enneagram. Featuring nine types, the Enneagram consists of three centers of intelligence—emotional or feeling, mental or thinking, and instinctual or gut. These correspond to the four temperaments in interesting ways, as you will see. Throughout the book, you will see your own temperament—and the temperaments of others in your life.

The Power of Insight

Knowledge of personality temperaments gives us a powerful, practical insight into human behavior that can have beneficial effects on our own lives and our day-to-day relationships. This information can help improve communication and pave the road to greater understanding and acceptance. When we see the behavior of others as simply *different* from our own—and not as "bad," "wrong," or "defective," we learn to see differences as simply differences, without judgment. Knowledge of temperament helps us live more harmoniously and productively with others, and increases the likelihood that we will give others what they *really* need or value, not what we *think* they need or value according to our self-referencing judgments.

We will also discover which people we naturally get along with, and which ones are more likely to push our buttons. It is common to be romantically attracted to people who have different temperaments from our own. We seem to have an instinctive need to look for the undeveloped or missing parts of ourselves in another person. But when the honeymoon wears off and we both start acting more like ourselves, the things that attracted us in the first place can start to grate on our nerves. After a while, our analytical and objective coworker can be seen as cold and impersonal; or the practical, dependable boyfriend suddenly becomes excruciatingly boring and predictable; or our creative business partner is revealed as unrealistic and impractical. With new insights, we can recognize these differences early on, and have a more realistic appreciation of what they offer.

At work, knowledge of temperament can help employers, employees, and coworkers improve relationships. It can also help people decide which work environments and professions might be best suited to their nature.

Parents can use their understanding of temperament to appreciate and encourage their children to be who they really are and develop their natural strengths and abilities—which is quite possibly the greatest gift we have to give to our children.

How to Get the Most Out of this Book

There is no "right" way to read this book—different personality temperaments are going to approach it in their own different ways. You might want to start by taking the temperament inventories to see which one best describes you. Some readers might then start from the beginning and read the book all the way through; others might estimate their temperament and go right to that description; and yet others might look for their partner's, friend's, or children's temperaments. Approach the material in whatever way feels most natural and comfortable to you.

To gain a true understanding of each temperament, take your time reading each of the chapters. Make it a process of observation and discovery. Each temperament has its own richness and can answer long-held questions about yourself and others.

And so, let's begin.

2 *

Personality Inventory

Which Temperament Type Are You?

Read each statement and use the following numbers to indicate your responses.

> 0–Not like me.
> 1–Somewhat like me.
> 2–Exactly like me.

Try to answer how you *really* are, not how you want to be or think you *should* be. Total all of your scores and mark them on the continuum on page 14.

Section 1

_0_ 1 I thrive in an orderly, organized environment with clearly defined rules and guidelines.

_2_ 2 I respect and honor the traditions, customs, and laws of society.

_0_ 3 I value being responsible, conscientious, and hard-working.

_1_ 4 I like to stick to standard ways of doing things. I am resistant to change.

_1_ 5 I can be a stickler for accuracy and details.

_2_ 6 I tend to worry about unpredictable events.

_1_ 7 I respect an organization's hierarchy and the chain of command.

_3_ 8 I am a loyal and dependable partner. I take my personal commitments seriously.

_2_ 9 Security, stability, and a sense of belonging are very important to me.

_1_ 10 I like to conserve my money and am willing to make financial sacrifices in the present for the sake of future security.

_2_ 11 I feel at ease in the traditional role of provider or homemaker.

_2_ 12 I value a partner who values family life as much as I do.

_2_ 13 I believe children should be well behaved, properly mannered, and respectful of their elders.

_1_ 14 I like jobs where performance is judged by explicitly stated criteria.

_1_ 15 I have the tendency to be controlling, inflexible, and closed-minded.

_2_ 16 Feeling useful and needed is very important to me.

_0_ 17 I value thoroughness and efficiency.

_0_ 18 I have difficulty being impulsive or spontaneous.

_1_ 19 I can have the tendency to instill guilt in others when they don't meet my expectations.

_0_ 20 I like to communicate about concrete, tangible, and observable information.

_23_ **TOTAL**

Section 2

_1_ 1 I tend to be optimistic, generous, fun-loving, and adventurous.

_2_ 2 I am spontaneous and trust my impulses to lead me in the right direction.

_2_ 3 I like to make work fun and exciting.

_1_ 4 I respond well to crisis situations but can lose interest once the crisis is over.

_2_ 5 I value my freedom and autonomy and don't like feeling restricted, confined, or controlled.

_2_ 6 I like spending money on the "good things in life" and can have trouble saving for the future.

_2_ 7 I am practical and pragmatic and like to see the daily tangible results of my work.

_1_ 8 I dislike wasting time talking about policies and procedures. I want to take immediate action.

_1_ 9 I like to experience all of what life has to offer. I don't want to miss out on anything.

_2_ 10 Setting long-term, abstract goals is not a priority for me.

_1_ 11 I believe that rules are meant to be changed and adapted to the needs of the moment.

_0_ 12 I take what people say at face value and am not interested in figuring out underlying motives or hidden meanings.

_1_ 13 I like risk and challenge.

_0_ 14 I love surprises and the unexpected, and thrive on last-minute changes.

___1___ 15 I like immediate gratification and I often leap before I look.

___1___ 16 As a child I was often too busy doing activities and having fun to take time to sit down and study.

___2___ 17 I dislike routine and overly structured work environments.

___1___ 18 I can be hyperactive and restless at times. I hate being bored.

___2___ 19 I value being flexible and adaptable.

___2___ 20 I value living in the present, in the here and now.

___27___ **TOTAL**

Section 3

___0___ 1 I am adept at developing, designing, and building models, theories, and systems.

___0___ 2 People would probably describe me as analytical, insightful, intellectual, or ingenious.

___2___ 3 I have strong convictions, trust my own judgments, and stand on principles no matter what the consequences.

___2___ 4 I value intelligence in myself and others and feel compelled to constantly improve my base of knowledge.

___0___ 5 I live for my work and intellectual pursuits. Relationships can take a backseat.

___0___ 6 I can be oblivious to social conventions and may forget to observe rituals such as anniversaries or birthdays.

___1___ 7 Dealing with day-to-day details and facts holds little interest for me.

___1___ 8 I can come across as a "know it all."

___1___ 9 I value independence and autonomy.

___0___ 10 I am skeptical and accept nothing on faith.

___8___ 11 I share connections of the mind more than those of the heart.

___0___ 12 I prefer a work environment that is based on objective and fair standards where achieving major goals and breakthroughs is part of the routine.

_0_ 13 I value efficiency in everything I do.

_1_ 14 I strive to make a unique contribution in my field of work.

_1_ 15 I am able to understand and synthesize complex information, see patterns and interconnections, anticipate future trends, and focus on long-range goals.

_1_ 16 I dislike hierarchy and bureaucratic structure.

_0_ 17 I like relating through mental challenges such as interesting discussions or debates, or games of chess and bridge.

_0_ 18 People sometimes see me as impersonal, detached, and aloof.

_0_ 19 I value logic, rationality, objectivity, and clear thinking.

_2_ 20 I don't shy away from critiquing or correcting people.

_12_ **TOTAL**

Section 4

_2_ 1 I value being warm-hearted, affirming, empathic, and compassionate.

_2_ 2 I value genuineness and authenticity in myself and others.

_2_ 3 I enjoy work that allows me to use my creativity and individuality. I am not content to just "make a living."

_1_ 4 I like to use my insight to benefit people and help them to realize their potential.

_2_ 5 I am curious and innovative and have a rich and active imagination.

_2_ 6 I enjoy sharing personal values, dreams, psychological and spiritual ideas, and new ways of seeing things.

_2_ 7 I can become self-absorbed in my search for identity and self-actualization.

_2_ 8 I invest a lot of effort, emotion, and enthusiasm in my relationships, sometimes more than a partner is comfortable with.

_2_ 9 I have a strong desire for harmony and am good at conflict resolution.

_2_ 10 - I can be too idealistic and independent-minded to work in most corporate, government, or military environments.

_2_ 11 I dream of having a deeply fulfilling, meaningful, and emotionally intense relationship with an "ideal" partner.

_2_ 12 I can be hypersensitive and take everything personally.

_2_ 13 I can become overly involved in other people's psyches and lives, and must guard against sympathizing with another's hurt beyond what the person is actually experiencing.

_2_ 14 I am interested in understanding and expressing my deepest feelings.

_2_ 15 I have a vision of an ideal world and want to work toward creating that vision here on earth.

_1_ 16 I am satisfied with the broad grasp of a subject without needing to master the facts or details.

_1_ 17 I often take sides with the underdog.

_2_ 18 After the initial challenge or newness disappears, I can get bored with a project.

_2_ 19 I dislike supervision and a lot of structure and rules.

_2_ 20 Working with people who don't encourage, appreciate, and affirm me can be very difficult. If I work with others it's important for me to feel encouraged and appreciated.

_38_ **TOTAL**

List your total for each type. The highest score indicates your strongest temperament tendencies.

Section 1: _26_ — Security Seeker

Section 2: _20_ — Experience Seeker

Section 3: _18_ — Knowledge Seeker

Section 4: _26_ — Ideal Seeker

Mark where you fall on each of the continuums.

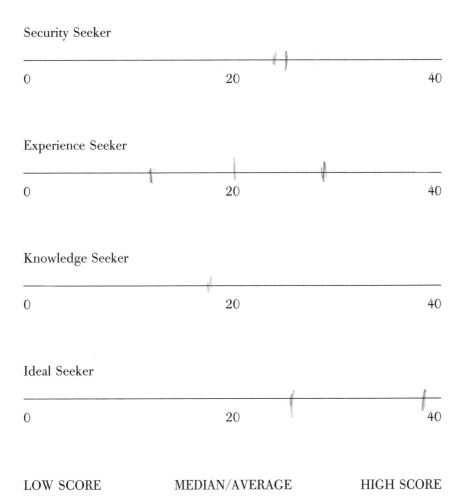

Security Seeker

0   20   40

Experience Seeker

0   20   40

Knowledge Seeker

0   20   40

Ideal Seeker

0   20   40

LOW SCORE   MEDIAN/AVERAGE   HIGH SCORE

This should give you an idea of your Temperament type, but read on to learn more about which one fits you best.

Identifying Your Temperament

If you came out with a significantly higher score on one particular temper-ament, you probably have found your right match. Read the chapter that describes this temperament to see how well it fits you. When people find their temperament, they are often surprised at how accurate it seems. Keep in mind, however, that not every word or sentence will describe you perfectly. If it fits at least 70 percent, it's probably the right one.

For some people, one temperament doesn't tell the whole story. Many people have a secondary one, and perhaps even a tertiary or third one. You will probably relate to bits and pieces of other temperaments, but one is your inborn temperament, the one most dominant in your personality.

Some people have difficulty finding their best temperament fit. There are several reasons for this. You may have answered the statements based on how you think you *should* be rather than on what your true nature *is*. Some people score high on a particular temperament if they think that is the "better" or the "right" way to be. This is especially true if you felt pressured by your family, or the community you grew up in, to behave in certain ways that were not your true nature. For example, in the United States the Security Seeker temperament is the most accepted style of behavior. Being dutiful, responsible, conscientious, and hardworking is the standard or rewarded way to be. If you are in a career or profession that requires skills that do not fit your true nature, you may be answering according to how you operate at work. Or perhaps you've arrived at a time in your life when you are focusing on developing other parts or aspects of yourself that are not related to your inborn nature. At midlife this is very common, as it is during periods of crisis such as a separation or divorce.

If you are having trouble identifying your temperament, keep track of your behavior for a few weeks. Notice your natural inclinations in different situations. To gain a real understanding of each temperament, take your time reading each of the chapters. Make it a process of self-observation and self-discovery.

3 *

Security Seekers

Approximately 40 percent of the U.S. Population

One never notices what has been done;
one can only see what remains to be done.
—MARIE CURIE

Security Seekers are motivated by the need to be responsible and dependable family members, friends, and employees. They are solid citizens, and they value being seen that way. Security Seekers feel obligated by their very nature to work hard and do their part. Being useful and doing their duty gives them a sense of self-respect and a feeling of belonging. Their need for responsibility or duty is so strong that they may take on too many responsibilities.

Security Seekers are the preservers of the social order. They honor and respect the customs, traditions, and social standards of the society and groups to which they belong—the family, community, or organization. Doing

so gives them a sense of safety and stability. It's not about tradition in the absolute sense, but the traditions of the group they are in.

Security Seekers trust and respect authority and the hierarchical order. Rules, regulations, and conformity make things stable and predictable and facilitate accountability. They know that change is inevitable, but they never opt for it at the expense of the tried and true.

Relationships

In their relationships, Security Seekers:

- are loyal and dependable mates. They take their obligations seriously and are willing to make sacrifices to honor their commitments.

- place a high value on home and family and bring stability to their relationship and home life.

- like the predictability of married life. They are the most marriage-minded of all the temperaments.

- are often comfortable in the traditional role of provider or homemaker.

- provide for their family's financial well-being and are willing to make sacrifices in the present for the sake of future security.

> ✳ A reminder to everyone spending money like there's
> no tomorrow. There is a tomorrow.
> —AD FOR CHASE MANHATTAN BANK

- focus on the day-to-day business of living and show caring by doing practical things—mowing the lawn, fixing the car, cooking, sewing, cleaning, paying the bills, and the like.

- show their love in traditional ways (gifts, cards, flowers, going to family or social gatherings).

- take pride in keeping the things they value well-cared for. Their possessions can be thought of as extensions or reflections of themselves.

- are organized and orderly and thrive on structure and routine.

> ✳ It is not in novelty but in habit that we find
> the greatest pleasure.
> —RAYMOND RADIGUET

- tend to observe the conventional or "proper" social etiquette when dating.

- often proceed cautiously about the business of courtship. They want to make a sound choice of a mate and not get caught up in their passions. Often favor long engagements.

- value social appropriateness.

- often have high expectations of how everyone and everything should be. They can be critical of needs or values that differ from their own.

- are sensible and down-to-earth.

Thinking-type Security Seekers are often direct and straightforward, and they sometimes overwhelm others with their bluntness. They can be insensitive of people's needs and feelings and how their remarks or judgments affect others. They are often unaware of their own feelings and emotional needs, especially their tender or vulnerable feelings. Expressing warmth can be difficult. About 65 percent of *Thinking*-type Security Seekers are male.

Feeling-type Security Seekers are sympathetic, caring, emotionally supportive, and concerned about other people's feelings. Being assertive or direct can be difficult for them. To have harmonious relationships, they tend to temper their judgments or keep them to themselves. About 65 percent of *Feeling*-type Security Seekers are female.

Security Seekers often do well in various kinds of relationships with other Security Seekers because they can feel supported in their strong need for tradition and dependability. It is common for the *Thinking* types to be in intimate relationships with *Feeling* types.

Communication

Security Seekers like to think and talk about concrete, tangible, observable information (prices, wages, food, clothing, recreation, people, children, time, the weather). When communicating, they like things to be stated clearly and specifically and to make sense. They are not drawn to search for hidden meanings or assumptions about things. They are impatient with theories and abstract or conceptual thinking, unless it can be applied in practical ways. Speculative thinking, or information that is vague, arbitrary, or impractical, holds little interest for them.

As Parents

As parents, Security Seekers:

- provide structure and consistency and take their parental role seriously. They want to set a good example for their children.

- can instill guilt when their children don't meet their expectations.

- see to it that their children have the "proper" social attitudes and behave correctly. They want their children's behavior to reflect well on them.

- often place importance on grades, college degrees, and traditional education, and encourage "practical" careers.

- tend to be overly protective and concerned about their children. They can project their worries onto their children, especially Security Seeker children, who have a natural tendency toward worry.

Security Seekers can be quick to rein in or punish unacceptable behavior such as laziness, complacency, lack of effort, and any form of rebelliousness or nonconformity. Their controlling nature can create rebelliousness in some children, especially those of other temperaments.

As Children and Teens

As children and teens, Security Seekers:

- are usually cooperative, respectful of authority, and want to please adults. They often respond to criticism or punishment by trying even harder.

- don't usually question the rules—*if* they make sense. They can have streaks of stubbornness if the rules don't make sense, however.

- are concerned about doing things the "right" way (chores, homework, and so on).

- often become responsible at an early age. They can sometimes act like a parent toward other children and even toward a parent.

- enjoy having visible signs of approval for their efforts—gold stars, trophies, good grades, perfect attendance.

- take well to traditional teaching methods (repetition and drill, workbooks, lecture) and learn best in a step-by-step approach.

- are drawn to practical subjects and learning useful skills (typing, math, shop, business subjects, college prep).

- often like participating in school and community activities (clubs, teams, scouts, student government) which give them a sense of belonging and affiliation.

- like being entrusted with responsibilities. They often have part-time jobs and save their money for clothes, a car, or college.

- thrive in a predictable and consistent environment with clearly defined guidelines.

- have trouble with ambiguity, uncertainty, and constant change. They like knowing that what is so today will be so tomorrow.

- expect the adults to be in charge. They can get frustrated, anxious, and upset if they can't get the guidance they need.

Because of their need to fit in, be accepted, and have their opinions be similar to those important to them, Security Seeker children are rarely rebellious. Rebelliousness is not predictable and shakes their sense of security. They can sometimes become involved in groups whose norms prescribe more risk-taking or rebellious behavior and do things they wouldn't necessarily do on their own. This is especially true for male Security Seekers who are expected to me more testy and "macho." Security Seeker parents may be less controlling with boys than girls because the traditional expectations for boys is for them to be more risk-taking and adventuresome. Girls are expected to be feminine or "ladylike."

Since approximately 40 percent of people in the United States are Security Seekers, the chances of their having at least one parent and many teachers who are of the same temperament are high. Elementary and secondary teachers tend to be Security Seekers. As a result, children who are Security Seekers often feel more understood than children of the other three temperaments while growing up.

At Work

If a task is once begun
Never leave it till it's done.
Be the labor great or small
Do it well or not at all.

—ANON

At work, Security Seekers:

- often like working in a well-established organization and focusing on the company's goals.

- value cooperation and working with others toward common goals.

- use their time and resources effectively and go to great lengths to get the job done.

- plan their work well in advance and have a realistic picture of how long it will take to complete tasks.

- like having things settled, decided, and completed.

- weigh things carefully and try to see the practical effects and consequences of their actions.

- excel at establishing and overseeing policies and standard operating procedures that provide stability, organization, and quality control.

- are good at seeing what is inconsistent or impractical and keeping things running smoothly and efficiently.

✴ Let all things be done decently and in order.

—CORINTHIANS 14:40

- value thoroughness and accuracy and pay attention to the details and the "fine print."

- like to stick to standard ways of doing things and are resistant to change. Risk is carefully weighed against the likelihood of success.

> ✳ **If it ain't broke, don't fix it.**
>
> —ANONYMOUS

- often have a formal or official style when dealing with colleagues until they get to know them.

- trust in and respect authority and the hierarchical order. They often aspire to be in positions of authority themselves (CEO, president, executive, manager, supervisor, administrator).

- believe that everyone can make something of themselves if they just work hard enough. They admire people who work their way up through the ranks and become successful.

- like jobs where performance is judged by explicitly stated criteria.

Extroverted Security Seekers often like working collaboratively with others in a stable and predictable environment, but one that has a variety of people. Some like being in charge and are often leaders.

Introverted Security Seekers often prefer working independently, behind the scenes. They like to work with a minimum of interruption and focus on one project or task. Although they tend to not seek leadership positions, they can make important contributions when they hold such positions.

Thinking-type Security Seekers work better with facts and numbers than with people. They tolerate the procedures and regulations of an institution but can be impatient with the individuals. They are skillful at organizing data in a systematic, logical way and applying the information practically. They are tough and firm, but fair.

Feeling-type Security Seekers are sensitive to and considerate of people's individual needs and prefer occupations where their warm and friendly nature is appreciated. They like working in a congenial, harmonious atmosphere where they can provide practical and tangible help to others. They thrive on being needed but can feel overburdened and stressed from taking care of others.

Careers

Security Seekers are well suited for a wide variety of career paths. The following list offers a sampling of occupations they often find satisfying given their strengths and abilities.

- **Health Care:** physical therapist, nurse, medical technician, speech pathologist, dentist, dental hygienist, physician, pharmacist, optometrist/optician, veterinarian, lab technician, dietitian/nutritionist, massage therapist, home health aid

- **Finance:** accountant, auditor, bank officer, financial manager, stockbroker

- **Clerical:** secretary, office manager, bookkeeper

- **Business/Sales/Service:** real estate agent, retail owner or salesperson, merchandise planner, telemarketer, insurance agent, security guard, credit counselor, cleaning person, beautician, flight attendant, special-events coordinator

- **Education/Social Service/Counseling:** teacher (preschool/elementary special education, mathematics, technical, trade), social worker, counselor (alcohol and drug addiction, guidance), religious educator, school principal, librarian, athletic coach, clergy, community welfare worker

- **Technical/Trades:** electrician, machinist, general contractor, farmer, technician, mechanic, construction worker, engineer

- **Managerial:** administrator, supervisor, manager

- **Legal/Civil Service:** government worker, military personnel, police/probation officer, fireman, attorney, paralegal, legal secretary, judge

- **Creative:** interior decorator, floral designer, artist, photographer, chef

- **Other professions:** computer programmer or operator, surveyor, botanist, geologist, marine biologist

Leisure

> ✳ It is impossible to enjoy idling thoroughly unless one has plenty of work to do.
>
> —JEROME K. JEROME

Security Seekers enjoy participating in the traditional forms of entertainment (theater, movies, sporting events, dining out) and they like having a good time when their work is done. They sometimes find it hard to relax because they prefer to be "productive." Even on vacation, they want to use their time well. Retirement and the empty nest can be difficult for some.

Security Seekers like getting things done and focusing on activities that have a practical purpose. They often spend time reading or taking classes to improve themselves. They usually lead very busy lives and are seldom bored. Many volunteer in church and community activities.

Security Seekers like observing and celebrating the traditional holidays, weddings, graduations, anniversaries, and birthdays with family and friends. They are often the social planners for the family.

The more *Extroverted* Security

Seekers especially like having an active lifestyle and often have a wide circle of friends. They can be entertaining and fun and have a good time when their work is done. Many are in charge of community service organizations and volunteer activities.

The more *Introverted* types are often modest, unassuming, and down to earth. They enjoy more quiet time to themselves and being one-on-one with a few long-term close friends. They often prefer low-key, planned activities and having time for their independent projects. They often have a rich inner world and a dry understated wit.

What's Hard About Being a Security Seeker

Security Seekers are stressed by:

- feeling burdened and obligated by too much responsibility. They can have difficulty saying no.

- having many "shoulds" and "oughts" for themselves and feeling guilty if they're not living up to their expectations.

- feeling unappreciated for all they do. Expressing hurt or resentment can be difficult, however.

- getting upset and resentful when others aren't working as hard as they are.

- not taking time to relax and have fun.

- feeling left out or that they don't belong or fit in.

- making mistakes and being criticized.

- worrying about the things that could go wrong (the big things—their health, jobs, homes, families, finances, inflation, and the standards of society, and the smaller things—getting the chores done, acting appropriately, being on time, the neighbor's lawn).

Peeves

Inefficiency

Wasting resources

Lack of respect/Insubordination/Rule breaking

Disorder/Sloppiness/Bad manners

Selfishness

Lack of integrity

Impulsivity/Unpredictability

Lack of common sense

Lack of discipline

Deadlines being ignored

Idle speculation

Flightiness/Flakiness

Apathy/Idleness

What Others Admire

People of other temperaments often think Security Seekers:

• are loyal and dependable.

• are there through the hard times and willing to go the extra mile.

• are responsible and trustworthy and do what they say they will do. Their word is their bond.

• are helpful and supportive in practical ways.

- have high standards, morals, and principles.

- are realistic, practical, steadfast, reliable, and down-to-earth.

- are organized and efficient and take care of the practical details of life.

- prepare well for crisis situations.

What Others Find Challenging

People of other temperaments sometimes think Security Seekers:

- have high expectations of how everyone and everything *should* be and try to get others to meet their standards. They can be critical of things that are not done according to accepted standards and may try to instill guilt when people don't do what they expect.

- can be closed-minded, self-righteous, and convinced their way is the only right way.

> ✳ When I married Mr. Right, I didn't know his first name
> was Always.
> —ANNE GILCHRIST

- can be sticklers for rules.

- can be overly cautious and resistant to change. They can hinder the creativity and innovativeness of others and create roadblocks and stagnation instead of progress and growth.

- can be pessimistic and worry about everything that could go wrong. They think people who don't worry are irresponsible. Their doubts and fears can be tiring to others.

- can forgive but rarely forget.

- can be stingy with money.

- can fail to appreciate and validate the effort of others because they think good work *should* be done as a matter of course, since that's what they expect of themselves.

This is especially true for the *Thinking*-type Security Seekers, who tend to be logical and analytical.

Things Security Seekers Would *Never* Dream of Doing

You'll never catch a Security Seeker:

- loafing watching television all weekend long, and feeling no guilt about doing so.

- allowing the kids to leave their rooms any way they want, even when company's coming.

- trusting that their off-the-cuff speech for the annual sales meeting will be just fine.

- letting their teenager dye her hair purple right before their twenty-fifth wedding anniversary party.

- buying a car without doing any comparison shopping.

- showing up at a potluck dinner empty-handed.

How to Get Along with Security Seekers

If you want to get along with Security Seekers:

- Express your appreciation and gratitude for all they do. Don't take them for granted. It's often difficult for them to ask for thanks because they feel it's their obligation and responsibility to work hard.

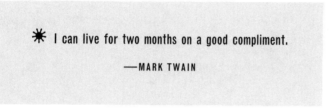

> ✳ I can live for two months on a good compliment.
>
> —MARK TWAIN

- Acknowledge them for being realistic, practical, organized, and efficient.

- Honor your commitments and do what you say you are going to do.

- Stand by them and be loyal and supportive.

- Show respect, even if they're not the authority.

- Respect their need for predictability. Keep in mind that open-ended plans, last-minute changes, or cancellations can be stressful for them.

- Be understanding about their resistance to change.

- Admit mistakes and express regret if you have done something wrong.

- Be punctual. They don't like to waste time.

- Show them the practical application of your ideas if you want them to be accepted.

- Invite them to participate in activities, projects, and plans. Security Seekers thrive on belonging.

- Ask for their advice and support. They often like playing the role of advisor and are good at demonstrating how things are done.

- Help them to loosen up and have fun.

- Don't take advantage of their tendency to take on an "extra load." Take your fair share of the responsibility so they don't end up with all the work.

> ✳ No woman ever shot her husband while he was
> doing the dishes.
> —ANONYMOUS

In addition to the comments above, the following suggestions can be particularly effective when dealing with Security Seeker children:

- Provide structure for them, even if it's just one or two routines a day to help them feel grounded, comfortable, and secure.

- When you assign them a task, give step-by-step instructions, guidelines, and time frames. Be clear about what is expected.

- When teaching, present your ideas in a sequential manner. Use specific and concrete examples and avoid going off on tangents.

- When you give them a chore, be sure the directions are clear and specific. Avoid complicated explanations.

- Offer them different sensory experiences (art projects, sandbox, clay, finger paints, simple cooking, gardening).

- Motivate them with special privileges and tangible rewards such as stars for perfect attendance, money or treats for doing household chores, and the like.

Security Seekers like concrete evidence that they are valued.

Practical Suggestions for Security Seekers

PERSONAL GROWTH AND SELF-DEVELOPMENT

- Make time for activities that are relaxing, fun, or personally satisfying.

- Be sure to use your allotted vacation time. And when you go away, leave all your work at home.

- Focus on what you *want* to do rather than on what you think you *should* do.

- Expand your sense of self to include more than what you *do* or produce.

- Don't wait for someone else to tell you that you did well. Pat yourself on the back.

- Be impulsive now and then and allow the more spontaneous sides of your personality to have expression.

- Be open to trying new ways of doing things. Avoid getting stuck in ruts.

- Learn to acknowledge or trust other ways of knowing, including hunches, dreams, and intuition.

- Practice focusing on the best things that could happen, instead of the worst.

> ✳ If you spend your whole life waiting for the storm, you'll
> never enjoy the sunshine.
>
> —MORRIS WEST

- Learn to trust yourself and your own insights rather than seeking answers from outside authorities.

RELATIONSHIPS

- Keep in mind that there is more than one way to do things. Do not assume that you know what's best for others. Refrain from telling people what they should and shouldn't do.

> ✳ The one thing more difficult than following a regimen is
> not imposing it on others.
>
> —MARCEL PROUST

- When dealing with children, avoid remarks such as "Because I said so. You don't need any more reason than that," or "Why can't you be more like your sister?"

- Avoid guilt-tripping others when your expectations are not met, or when you feel taken for granted.

- Beware of being overly cautious or rigid in your thinking. Don't rule out other people's ideas because you consider them unrealistic or impractical.

- Keep in mind that stability, security, and routine may feel confining and boring to people who prefer more variety, creativity, excitement, and surprise.

- Beware of rescuing irresponsible or dependent people. Realize that you can be supportive of others without *doing* things for them.

- Avoid staying in unhealthy relationships out of a sense of duty and obligation. Get help in ending inappropriate relationships.

- Express appreciation to others for their efforts, even for the small things they do. Make it a rule to mention what is done well, not merely what needs correcting or improving.

WORK

- Avoid taking on extra work. Learn to say no. Don't try to do too much because you'll risk becoming resentful, stressed, or exhausted. Speak up if you feel you are being treated unfairly or being taken advantage of.

- Be sure to delegate, so that others can help.

- Develop flexibility and be willing to make positive changes in operating procedures.

- Set realistic limits for yourself and learn what "good enough" means. Allow room for mistakes.

- Don't be in such a hurry to have matters settled and decided. Slow down the decision-making process.

Famous Security Seekers

- **Service People:** Mother Teresa, Florence Nightingale, Billy Graham

- **Entertainers and Media Personalities:** Judge Judy, Dr. Laura Schlessinger, Felix Unger of *The Odd Couple*, Lucy in *Peanuts*, Radar on *M*A*S*H*, Kathie Lee Gifford, Bryant Gumbel, Arnold Schwarzenegger, Archie Bunker, Mike Wallace, Dan Rather

- **Presidents/Politicians:** George Washington, Calvin Coolidge, James Polk, Andrew Johnson, Harry S. Truman, Gerald Ford, Woodrow Wilson, George Bush, Sr., Rush Limbaugh, Ross Perot, General Colin Powell, Ken Starr, Janet Reno, Oliver North, Condaleeza Rice

- **First Ladies:** Barbara Bush, Nancy Reagan, Laura Bush

- **Business Tycoons:** Andrew Carnegie, John D. Rockefeller, Henry Ford

4

Experience Seekers

Approximately 40 percent of the U.S. Population

All I can say about life is, oh God, enjoy it.
—BOB NEWHART

Experience Seekers are motivated by the need to act spontaneously on their impulses—not just for fun, but for problem solving as well. Experience Seekers live in the present, in the here and now. The past holds little or no excitement; the future is too far away and intangible. Experience Seekers value stimulation and excitement, and are always on the lookout for some new experience or adventure. They value their freedom and independence and don't like to be burdened by obligation, duty, or confining promises. If people try to change them or tell them what to do, they can be rebellious. Experience Seekers often do well—and actually thrive—in crisis situations because these call on their ability to act spontaneously and skillfully in the moment. Some are drawn to risk and challenge. They value and admire competence and skill in performance, both in themselves and others, and they want their actions to have an impact. Many are agile and well-coordinated.

Relationships

In their relationships, Experience Seekers:

- like being with people who share their interests or give them freedom to do their own thing.

- are generous and like giving for the fun of it, or to make others happy. They don't necessarily expect anything in return.

- are often more comfortable expressing caring or affection through action rather than through words (fixing things, helping to make things happen, solving problems, doing things for others).

- like variety, experimentation, and surprise, and doing things unconventionally much of the time.

- tend to be flexible and adaptable.

- are keen observers of human behavior. They can sense where people are coming from and are good at predicting what they will do.

- often appear optimistic and cheerful. Many Experience Seekers consider themselves "realists" versus "optimists." Optimism implies possibility while realism suggests what "is."

- prefer to keep things light and upbeat. Experience Seekers don't like being too serious.

- want to experience life directly rather than discuss its meaning.

- can withdraw, tune out, or walk away from relationships that they experience as unexciting, boring, or filled with tension and conflict.

- don't spend much time thinking or worrying about the quality of their relationships; they are too busy living their lives.

- sometimes feel trapped by obligation and commitment.

> ✻ Marriage is a great institution, but I'm not ready
> for an institution.
> —MAE WEST

Thinking-type Experience Seekers can be very direct and straightforward, or even blunt. They can be impersonal and cool, and sometimes miss the emotional side of things. Some are insensitive or unaware of the emotional impact of their behavior on others. Expressing their love, appreciation, and tenderness can be difficult. They are most often male (about 65 percent).

Feeling-type Experience Seekers are more sympathetic, caring, and concerned about other people's feelings. Because they want their relationships to be harmonious, they tend to avoid confrontation and conflict. They are most often female (about 65 percent).

Communication

Experience Seekers prefer talking about practical, concrete, tangible, and realistic things (the weather, sports, food, clothing, recreation, people). When a discussion seems abstract or theoretical, they can get impatient and lose interest. Experience Seekers take what people say literally, at face value, and are not interested in figuring out hidden or underlying meanings. They often think that speculative thinking about what might be, or could be, is a waste of time. Experience Seekers tend to communicate with an easy, informal style, and their language tends to be uncomplicated.

As Parents

As parents, Experience Seekers:

- like to expose their children to many adventures and experiences, and encourage them to be physically active.

- can be playful and enjoy having fun with their children.

- often value boldness and courage. They can sometimes be impatient with a child who seems timid.

- often give their children the freedom and autonomy to do their own thing, sometimes more than the child can handle.

- can be permissive and fail to provide consistency or discipline for their children. They can sometimes be more like a playmate than a parent.

As Children and Teens

As children and teens, Experience Seekers:

- learn best in an action-centered, hands-on environment that stimulates their senses (building, playing musical instruments, participating in sports, dance, painting, arts and crafts, woodwork, metal shop, cooking, sewing). Regimented classroom settings do not work well for Experience Seekers.

- like to learn subjects that are practical and relevant to their interests. They are usually not interested in learning for its own sake.

- are often too busy having fun to take the time to sit down and study.

- have little interest in theoretical or abstract subjects unless they can be used for doing something practical.

- can be impulsive and leap before they look.

- like variety and often jump from one activity to another. However, they can also devote a lot of time and effort to achieving skill in their areas of interest.

- can sometimes have trouble keeping things organized and orderly unless it's something that's interesting to them, like their hobbies.

- want to do things in their own time and in their own way. They usually don't like being told how to do something. They often don't read the directions.

- often have boundless energy. Some can be full of fun and mischief. When they are bored, they can get restless or disruptive and stir things up. They can sometimes exasperate their parents or teachers with their indifference to scolding or reprimanding. (This is especially true of the *Thinking*-type and *Extroverted* Experience Seekers.)

- can leave school or home early in life, in order to be independent and on their own. Some return to school only if they see that an education will be useful.

Even though four out of ten children (40 percent) in a classroom are Experience Seekers, their natural talents and abilities are often overlooked and undeveloped in traditional schools, which are run primarily by Security Seekers. The sit-down, follow the rules, speak-when-spoken-to, lecture-type teaching methods go against the nature of the Experience Seekers. They often feel out of step or disenchanted with school as they move up through the grades, because the higher the grade level, the more abstract the curriculum gets. Rather than meeting their needs for a more action-centered, hands-on curriculum, teachers sometimes label them hyperactive. Sometimes they are diagnosed as having Attention Deficit Disorder (ADD), and given drugs to calm them down. Experience Seeker children sometimes underestimate themselves and suffer from low self-esteem or decide not to pursue advanced education, because the school curriculum does not recognize their natural gifts.

> ✳ All too often kids are labeled because someone is confusing a need for a different teaching method with a "learning problem."
> —MARIAEMMA PELOLLO-WILLIS

At Work

At work, Experience Seekers:

- want their work to be exciting, fun, and challenging.

- often like frequent change of tasks and having many projects going on at once. They can become restless and bored when their work is not full of variety.

- often do well in crisis situations because they are quick to respond to the needs of the moment. They can lose interest when things settle down and return to "normal."

- want to get tasks done as fast as possible so they can move on to something they prefer doing.

- prefer a loosely structured environment where they have leeway to do things their own way.

- are adept at assessing a situation, coming up with a variety of solutions, and taking the necessary actions to achieve the desired outcome.

- dislike spending a lot of time contemplating or talking about things.

✳ Good instinct usually tells you what to do long before your head has figured it out.

—MICHAEL BURKE

- are not very interested in setting long-term abstract goals or in planning for the future.

- are realistic and pragmatic and like work that delivers practical results.

- like working in a cooperative, egalitarian environment. The less authority the better.

- feel restricted by excessive rules, inflexible structure, and hierarchy. They tend to bypass policies, regulations, and bureaucratic red tape if they think they will get in the way of getting things done.

- are not usually impressed with status or degrees.

Extroverted Experience Seekers like working in a lively, stimulating environment with energetic people and having many projects going on at once. They often like working as part of a team and some are good at dealing with the public. Many are persuasive, good at motivating others and promoting themselves.

Introverted Experience Seekers often prefer working alone, behind the scenes. They have little need to directly influence or control. They can bring a certain sense of quiet, playful enthusiasm to the work environment.

Thinking-type Experience Seekers are skillful at organizing facts and data in a logical way and applying the information practically. They deal with concrete problems expediently and don't waste effort on the unnecessary. Resourceful, pragmatic, and results-oriented, they are often good at troubleshooting.

Feeling-type Experience Seekers usually enjoy careers where their warm and friendly nature will be appreciated and where they can be of practical service to others. They thrive in a supportive, affirming, adaptable environment where there is little interpersonal conflict. Work that is gratifying and consistent with their personal or inner values is important.

Careers

Experience Seekers can excel at many careers. The following list is just a sampling of some occupations they tend to excel at.

- **Technical/Trades:** general contractor, construction worker, carpenter, machinist, electrician, mechanic, farmer, computer programmer, surveyor, botanist, geologist, marine biologist, electrical engineer

- **Sports:** professional athlete, coach, fitness instructor, recreation leader, sportscaster

- **Entertainment:** dancer, musician, actor, composer, singer, news reporter, film producer

- **Creative:** craftsman, artisan, artist, photographer, designer (fashion, floral, landscape, interior), jeweler, gardener, chef

- **Sales/Service:** real estate broker, agent, sales (retail, travel, sports equipment, health care), sales representative, merchandise planner, storekeeper, promoter, entrepreneur, special-events coordinator, fundraiser, public relations specialist, bartender/waiter, gardener, beautician

- **Travel/Transportation services:** flight attendant, tour guide, transportation operators, pilot

- **Civil Service:** police officer, firefighter, military serviceman, forest ranger

- **Health care:** nurse, dental/medical assistant, paramedic, veterinarian, physical therapist, physician, optician/optometrist, radiological/X-ray technician, massage therapist, nutritionist, home health aid

- **Education/Social service:** teacher (early childhood/elementary, PE, drama, special education), child-care worker, dance and movement therapist, counselor (alcohol and drug addiction), probation officer

- **Other professions:** finance (securities analyst, auditor, stockbroker, banker, investor, bookkeeper), attorney, paralegal, private investigator, hunter, race car driver

Leisure

> ✳ Life is about enjoying yourself and having a good time.
>
> —CHER

Many Experience Seekers have interests and hobbies that they avidly pursue (painting, building, cooking, home or car repair, crafts, decorating, sewing, music). They often take pride in being able to do many things well. Some enjoy risk-taking, adrenaline-producing adventures (mountain climbing, skiing, hunting, skydiving, snowboarding, racing, surfing, rock climbing, speed boating, river rafting). Others prefer more low-key but still active hobbies (hiking, running, swimming, sailing, gardening camping). Most enjoy traveling and being on the go. They often like spending their money on music, dance, food, drink, entertainment, and shopping.

> ✳ Spend all you have before you die; do not outlive yourself.
>
> —GEORGE BERNARD SHAW

The outgoing, *Extroverted* Experience Seekers enjoy being around people. They can turn any occasion into a party. Some like telling stories, saying outrageous things, and being center stage. They can sometimes leave others feeling overwhelmed by their outgoing, enthusiastic, buoyant nature.

> ✴ We cherish our friends not for their ability to amuse us,
> but for ours to amuse them.
> —EVELYN WAUGH

The more reserved, *Introverted* Experience Seekers usually like being out in the world, but they also enjoy having time for quieter pursuits and being with a few close friends with whom they share common interests. They are private about expressing their thoughts and feelings, except with those close to them. For these introverts, "Actions speak louder than words."

What's Hard About Being an Experience Seeker

Experience Seekers are challenged by:

- being in the same place, with the same people, doing the same thing, day after day.

> ✴ Any idiot can face a crisis—it's this day-to-day living
> that wears you out.
> —ANTON CHEKHOV

- feeling restricted or constrained when they can't act spontaneously on their impulses.

- feeling bored, restless, or frustrated when they don't have a direction to channel their energy.

- procrastinating when they need to do things that are unexciting or unappealing, and then facing the negative consequences.

- feeling confined by other people's expectations.

- performing awkwardly, cowardly, or timidly.

- dealing with interpersonal conflicts.

Peeves

Overly serious or uptight people
Pessimism
Hierarchical structure
All talk and no action
Being told what to do and how to do it
Needy or dependent people

What Others Admire

People of other temperaments often think Experience Seekers:

- are open-minded and adaptable and not set in their ways.

- help people stay in touch with the here and now.

- are fun-loving and exciting companions. Their joy of life can be infectious (this is particularly true for *extroverted* Experience Seekers).

- like doing things no one else has thought of, or dared to try.

- are able to amuse and distract others from overly serious concerns.

- don't waste a lot of time looking back or mourning their losses.

- are ingenious and resourceful in solving immediate or practical problems.

- are very loyal to those who are loyal to them.

- are able to encourage others through in hard times.

- are good at improvising and pulling things together at the last minute.

- are easygoing, casual, and down-to-earth.

What Others Find Challenging

People of other temperaments sometimes think Experience Seekers:

- are resistant to committing to things and hard to pin down.

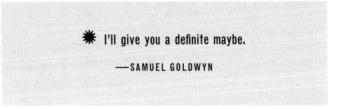

✳ I'll give you a definite maybe.

—SAMUEL GOLDWYN

- change their plans when new options present themselves, even if it means disappointing others.

- appear to go along with people's expectations, but they usually end up doing what they want.

- are impetuous, impulsive, and sometimes compulsive in their pursuit of pleasure.

- can be reckless in their risk-taking.

> ✳ The moment somebody says to me, "This is very risky," is the moment it becomes attractive to me.
>
> —KATE CAPSHAW

- can be unavailable or too busy for quiet times together.

- avoid dealing with negative feelings and interpersonal conflicts; can sometimes try to sweep problems under the rug.

- can be resistant to authority.

> ✳ I believe in a lively disrespect for most forms of authority.
>
> —RITA MAE BROWN

- don't always finish what they start, or follow through on commitments.

Things Experience Seekers Would
Never Dream of Doing:

You'll never catch an Experience Seeker:

- insisting on going for counseling when they're having marital problems.

- deciding on an exact itinerary for their entire vacation and sticking to it.

- choosing to spend their two-week summer holiday at a silent meditation retreat.

- volunteering to work on the Policy and Rules committee at work.

- passing up an invitation to go on a weekend getaway with a friend because they'd promised themselves they'd organize their office.

- finishing one project before starting another.

- making a to-do list each morning and following it to a T.

How to Get Along with
Experience Seekers

If you want to get along with Experience Seekers:

- Keep your relationship interesting and exciting. Surprise them; do the unexpected from time to time.

- Join in their activities and adventures.

- Appreciate their enthusiasm, spontaneity, and the enjoyment they get in the pleasures and fun of everyday experiences.

- Don't try to change them or tell them what to do. They are not likely to adapt to your needs.

- Don't try to pin them down or box them into too many schedules and routines. Give them as much leeway and freedom as you can.

- When making a request, give them several choices and alternatives, and then let go of your expectations.

- When making a point, use specific, concrete examples and guidelines, and stick to the facts and issues at hand. Pinpoint specific problems you're having and set aside a *limited* time to discuss them.

- Don't take yourself too seriously. Avoid too much analyzing and processing of feelings.

- Let them take more responsibility for the areas they feel are important, and less in areas they don't care much about.

- Let them know when it's *really* important that they follow through and stick with commitments or agreed-upon plans.

In addition to the above suggestions, the following might be helpful with Experience Seeker children:

- Don't expect them to sit still for long. Let them take breaks from home-work and chores. Break up car trips.

- Make learning active, exciting, and fun. Offer many opportunities for movement and hands-on activities.

- Try to make a game out of everyday chores and activities. Put on music and dance while you clean together, for example.

- Try to respond promptly to their requests.

- Build in some immediate and tangible rewards for tasks completed (money, treats, outings to their favorite places).

- Keep imperatives such as *sit still, do your homework, study hard, observe the rules,* and *clean your room* to a minimum.

- When discipline is necessary, make it immediate. When possible, remove the source of temptation.

- Avoid lectures. Say things clearly and get right to the point.

- Instead of telling them how to do something, engage them by asking them to help you do it.

- Help them find extracurricular activities (sports, music, dance, theater) in which they can excel.

- Find constructive outlets for their high physical energy.

- Help them develop time-management skills. Use positive reinforcement to help them stay on schedule.

- Give them a chance to show off and shine in action.

- Praise and applaud them for their strengths and talents.

Practical Suggestions for Experience Seekers

PERSONAL GROWTH AND SELF-DEVELOPMENT

- Avoid overextending, overindulging, or excess stimulation. Become aware of using activities such as drinking, overeating, compulsive spending, or watching TV that you might be using as diversions to avoid conflict or unpleasant situations.

- Take the time to reflect upon your experiences in order to see which ones are valuable to you. If you feel unfulfilled, try to find new interests or activities that you might find more satisfying.

- Spend some time thinking about your long-terms goals—what you want out of life five, ten, or twenty years from now.

- Learn to enjoy the deeper and quieter aspects of life, not just the highs and excitements. This is especially true for *Extroverted* Experience Seekers.

- Talk through your problems with someone you trust so that stress doesn't build up.

- Consider having one day a week to take care of the everyday business of life. This could vary from week to week.

- Before engaging in risky activities, consider the consequences of your actions.

> ✳ Experience is a good teacher, but she sends in terrific bills.
>
> —MINNA ANTRIUM

RELATIONSHIPS

- Make an extra effort to express in words your appreciation for what others do, including the little things.

- Keep in mind that variety, excitement, and adventure are not appealing to everyone. Some people prefer consistency and stability.

- Be mindful of your children doing activities they don't necessarily enjoy just to please you.

- Let others know up front about your need for freedom and autonomy. Incorporate some sense of freedom into the agreements you make with others so that you'll be better able to maintain your commitments to them. For example, married Experience Seekers might do best with money if they have some shared and some of their own to spend.

- Avoid making promises to change that you know you cannot fulfill.

- Do not ignore troubling situations in the hopes that they will go away. It's better to address issues as they come up than to let them accumulate.

- When you're ready to end a relationship, be honest rather than walking away without explanation.

- Avoid getting so caught up in the activities you love that you neglect your friends and loved ones.

WORK

- Resist the urge to deal only with immediate problems instead of less exciting but important tasks.

- If you have the tendency to leave projects unfinished or goals unmet, develop follow-through skills in order to gain a sense of completion and accomplishment.

- If you want to gain the respect of others at work, be mindful of the accepted ways of doing things and be willing to go through established channels. Sometimes, that is the most efficient way to get something done, even if it's less exciting.

- Take time to analyze your mistakes in order to avoid repeating them.

- Rather than choosing a career that takes the least amount of hard work, be willing to postpone some present gratificaton to find work that is truly fulfilling.

Famous Experience Seekers

- **Entertainers:** Elvis Presley, Judy Garland, Cher, Frank Sinatra, Jack Nicholson, Clint Eastwood, Mel Brooks, Jonathan Winters, Edith Bunker, Melanie Griffith, Chris Farley

- **Artists/Composers/Dancers/Musicians:** Paul Gauguin, Pablo Picasso, Wolfgang Amadeus Mozart, Martha Graham, Gene Kelly, Rod Stewart, Mick Jagger, Louis Armstrong, Woody Guthrie, Janis Joplin, Kenny Rogers, Willie Nelson

- **Writers:** Tennessee Williams, Ernest Hemingway, F. Scott Fitzgerald

- **Sports Figures:** Joe Namath, "Magic" Johnson, Michael Jordan, Mike Tyson, Babe Ruth, Mary Lou Retton, Scott Hamilton, Dennis Rodman

- **Presidents/Politicians:** John F. Kennedy, Lyndon Johnson, Theodore Roosevelt, Ted Kennedy, Winston Churchill, Jessie Ventura, George W. Bush.

- **Explorers/Adventurers:** Charles Lindbergh, Amelia Earhart

- **Other Famous Experience Seekers:** St. Francis of Assisi, Diana, Princess of Wales

5 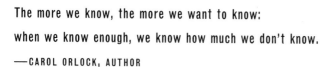 *

Knowledge Seekers

Approximately 10 percent of the U.S. population

The more we know, the more we want to know;
when we know enough, we know how much we don't know.
—CAROL ORLOCK, AUTHOR

Knowledge Seekers are motivated by the need for competency and information. They seek to understand the aspects of the world to which they are drawn, and to examine its universal truths and principles. Knowledge Seekers trust their ability to gather information through their intuition, which allows them to see patterns and connections and the relationships between things. Knowledge Seekers are often ingenious at conceptualizing, analyzing, and synthesizing complex information. They thrive on developing and designing theories and systems, and they focus on possibilities and long-range goals. Knowledge Seekers value objectivity and logical consistency, and are most likely to be convinced by solid reasoning. They have a strong resolve to accomplish the things they set their minds on, and they strive for self-mastery and improvement in everything they do.

Knowledge Seekers want to be in control of their own lives, and live according to their own standards. They are the most autonomous and independent-minded of all the temperaments, and they value being seen that way.

Relationships

In their relationships, Knowledge Seekers:

- like being intellectually challenged by the people around them. They see relationships as opportunities for learning. They enjoy connections of the mind, often even more than those of the heart, and are sometimes "mind mates" more than "soul mates."

- like to remain calm, cool, and level-headed. They do not want to be controlled by their emotions, spontaneous impulses, urges, or desires because that could lead to making mistakes or looking foolish.

- can have intense and passionate feelings but can be reserved about showing them. They are more comfortable expressing their thoughts than their feelings.

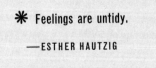

✳ **Feelings are untidy.**

—ESTHER HAUTZIG

- are sensitive to rejection but often hide their vulnerability with a show of coolness and detachment. They can feel deeply but tend to let their guard down only with people they trust.

- can be very loyal and supportive mates and friends.

- make every effort to uphold their commitments.

- show their caring in subtle ways—by helping others solve problems, mentoring, empowering others to develop their skills and potential, and by doing things for others.

- are often absorbed in the world of conceptual ideas and can live for their work and intellectual pursuits. They sometimes forget how much they need the nourishment of relationships.

- value change, learning, and growth as integral aspects of their relationships.

- tend to develop intimate relationships cautiously and slowly.

> ✳ True friendship is a plant of slow growth.
> —GEORGE WASHINGTON

- often prefer a partner who is independent and self-reliant, who doesn't depend on them for wholeness or happiness. They may choose a partner who handles the practical, day-to-day chores of domestic life, leaving them free to pursue their work.

- seek to maintain their independence and autonomy, and resist being manipulated or controlled.

- are not usually focused on acquiring material things beyond the necessities for basic security or comfort, with the exception of technological gadgets and books.

- can be oblivious to appearances.

- dislike spending time or energy making social connections or small talk. Finding a person they feel is worthy of making a personal commitment to can take a while, especially for introverted Knowledge Seekers.

Knowledge Seekers often do well in friendships and work relationships with other Knowledge Seekers, because they can satisfy each other's strong need for intellectual challenge. In their intimate relationships, they are more likely to choose mates of other temperaments.

In our culture, it is easier to be a male Knowledge Seeker than a female Knowledge Seeker because men are socialized to be logical, rational, independent, and direct—the traits that characterize this temperament. Female Knowledge Seekers are sometimes seen as "unfeminine" because their traits are more stereotypically male, including being, competitive, opinionated, and even argumentative. They often have less need to nurture and caretake than more "traditional" women. Female Knowledge Seekers often grow up hearing that "real" women are nurturing, sensitive, and compassionate, and thus they feel they must learn to develop their softer side. They may have limited choices in finding an intellectually stimulating partner because male Knowledge Seekers are often attracted to women of other temperaments.

Extroverted Knowledge Seekers are more gregarious, talkative, and can be engaging conversationalists with many interesting ideas and a wide-ranging repertoire of knowledge to draw from.

Introverted Knowledge Seekers prefer spending time alone to pursue their interests, and can feel invaded and intruded upon from too much contact with others. They prefer low-key, intimate, one-on-one social time. They are sometimes attracted to more outgoing partners who provide a bridge to the outside world. However, being with an introverted partner who is comfortable with silences and quiet time can also be appealing.

Communication

Knowledge Seekers prefer thinking and communicating about abstract, conceptual, impersonal events and ideas. They are oriented toward talking about possibilities rather than realities. Talking about concrete or factual matters, or the details and specifics of life, holds little interest for them and drains their energy. When speaking, they often state things coherently, articulately, precisely, and concisely. They tend to notice inconsistencies, contradictions, and logical flaws in their own and others' thinking and speech. Their language tends to be scholarly, complex, and occasionally obscure, and reflects their theoretical approach to life. Their thoughts move quickly from specifics to larger patterns and interconnections. When describing something they "see," they tend to jump from one thought to the next to wherever their intuition takes them. Despite their precise articulation, their ideas can be difficult for people of other temperaments to understand.

As Parents

As parents, Knowledge Seekers:

- place strong value on learning and self-improvement. They expect their children to challenge themselves intellectually.

- foster self-reliance in their children, so they grow up expressing independent thought and action.

- encourage their children to take responsibility for themselves, sometimes before the children are ready.

- sometimes have trouble expressing warmth and affection to their children.

- tend to take family responsibilities seriously, but can be so busy with their work and intellectual interests, that they neglect the day-to-day tasks of family life. They are sometimes bystanders rather than participants.

Some Knowledge Seekers are rigid, controlling, and demanding parents, and they place unrealistic expectations on their children.

Other Knowledge Seekers are more patient and accepting, sharing their insights while maintaining a more relaxed "live and let live" attitude.

As Children and Teens

As children and teens, Knowledge Seekers:

- are bright, clever, and challenged by learning. They are often labeled as bookworms or brains. Their intellectual development usually proceeds at a faster rate than their social development.

- will become bored if not mentally stimulated, or if their activities don't have some element of challenge.

- are constantly investigating and experimenting, striving to understand how things work. They often like taking things apart and putting them back together (construction sets, chemistry sets, erector sets, models). They are really scientists at heart.

- are curious and inquisitive and ask a lot of how and why questions—not to annoy adults, but because they really want to know the answers.

- often enjoy documenting and classifying their collections (coins, stamps, rocks, photos, toy soldiers or dolls, special treasures, etc.) but can be casual or neglectful of their rooms and day-to-day chores.

> ✳ One of the advantages of being disorderly is that one is
> constantly making exciting discoveries.
>
> —A. A. MILNE

- are fascinated by fantasy and science fiction stories, as well as biographies about inventors, scientists, and explorers.

- seek to be independent and self-sufficient, to think and act for themselves.

- often have little or no interest in developing social graces or being popular. Many prefer books and computers to school dances and football games. (This is especially true for *Introverted* Knowledge Seekers.)

- dislike being financially dependent as they get older because it diminishes autonomy and self-responsibility.

- will go along with the rules and authority *if* they believe they make sense, but they always want to know the reasons for requirements such as following the dress code, writing thank-you notes, doing chores, and the like.

- are very sensitive to being treated unjustly or unfairly.

- will work hard for teachers they respect.

Some Knowledge Seekers are high achievers and at the top of their class. Others feel that school is a waste of time and are not interested in grades. The latter group are often on their own in learning because the school curriculum is not geared to them until they reach college. College is usually more challenging and rewarding because they have more intellectual independence and can find other Knowledge Seekers to relate to, including their professors, who are often Knowledge Seekers themselves.

At Work

At work, Knowledge Seekers:

- have high standards of intellectual and professional competence, coupled with a strong determination to achieve long-term and short-term success in their field. However, their own feelings of success and achievement are more important to them than external accolades.

> ✳ There is no such thing as a great talent
> without great willpower.
> —HONORÉ DE BALZAC

- pride themselves for their innovativeness, ingenuity, and intuitive insights.

- are highly focused and can concentrate well.

- are quick to grasp complex situations, see interconnections, analyze implications, and identify alternative solutions.

- are resourceful in solving challenging problems and inventing new ways of doing things, with little patience for traditional approaches. Creating new systems is more important to them than applying past experience or existing knowledge.

- are pragmatic and seek to improve the efficient operation of systems. They are always on the lookout for error and wasted effort.

- use logical analysis to see how the facts serve their purpose of discovering new possibilities. They value facts only as evidence or examples of theory, not for their own sake.

- prefer working with strong-minded, independent people whom they respect, in a calm, conflict-free environment, with evaluations based on objective and fair standards.

- trust their own judgments and stand on principles no matter what the consequences.

- are not impressed with status, titles, credentials, celebrity, or other marks of social approval. Authorities have to prove themselves worthy of respect.

- dislike hierarchy and bureaucracy. They prefer consultative relationships over hierarchical ones. They will follow policies, rules, and procedures only *if* these make sense and are compatible with their values and goals.

- dislike taking instructions or advice unless the other is seen as having equal or greater knowledge or competence. They can be argumentative and opinionated when information from authorities contradicts what they believe to be true.

> ✳ Every great advance in natural knowledge has involved the
> absolute rejection of authority.
> —THOMAS HENRY HUXLEY

Some Knowledge Seekers are highly organized, decisive, and result-oriented. They enjoy applying their theories to see how well they work. Others are more focused on devising new projects and processes, and prefer leaving the application and implementation to others.

Some Knowledge Seekers like administering and being in charge as change-oriented leaders. Others prefer working independently, behind the scenes.

Careers

Many different careers are suitable for Knowledge Seekers. The following is a list of some occupations that have proven to be satisfying for many because their strengths and abilities are being utilized.

- **Education**: teacher/professor (science, economics, philosophy, psychology), curriculum designer, education consultant, administrator, historian, mathematician, research and development specialist, librarian

- **Medicine**: physician, psychiatrist, psychologist, health consultant, researcher

- **Sciences/Engineering**: scientist (biologist, chemist, physicist), archaeologist, astronomer, software developer, engineer, inventor

- **Business**: real estate developer, business owner/manager, management consultant, entrepreneur

- **Finance**: systems analyst, economist, financial planner, stockbroker, investment or business analyst, mortgage broker

- **Creative**: architect, photographer, artist, graphic designer, advertising director, actor, writer, editor, journalist, public speaker

- **Other professions**: administrator, attorney, labor relations worker, corporate team trainer, organizational development consultant, public relations specialist, environmental planner, computer programmer/analyst.

Leisure

> ✳ People say that life is the thing, but I prefer reading.
>
> —LOGAN PEARSALL SMITH

Knowledge Seekers strive for proficiency and competency at whatever activity they engage in, whether in work or leisure. Socializing for its own sake is not usually appealing, unless they can learn something in the process. Knowledge Seekers often enjoy intellectual exchanges and debating many sides of an issue. Friendships often revolve around shared expertise and intellectual integrity. Some enjoy games of mental strategy such as bridge and chess. Many enjoy attending lectures, readings, films, and cultural events, and going to museums.

What's Hard About Being a Knowledge Seeker

Knowledge Seekers are stressed by:

- obstacles that stand between them and their goals.

- feelings of inadequacy or self-doubt about their capabilities or accomplishments. They are the most self-critical of all the temperaments regarding their abilities.

- not being recognized for their true level of competency.

- overworking and forgetting their bodily needs.

> ✳ The chief function of the body is to carry the
> brain around.
> —THOMAS ALVA EDISON

- feeling powerless or out of control.

- unexpected displays of emotion (theirs' or others').

- routine or repetitive tasks, tight supervision, obsolete policies and procedures.

- being micromanaged.

Peeves

Demanding or controlling people
Inefficiency
Needy or clingy people
Meaningless or superficial chatter
Incompetence
People who are resistant to change
People who aren't inspired by a vision or who don't see the big picture

What Others Admire

People of other temperaments often view Knowledge Seekers as:

- intelligent, brilliant, and ingenious.

- alert and able to challenge others intellectually, especially other Knowledge Seekers.

- creative, innovative, and original thinkers who see things from a broad perspective and contribute greatly to unexplored aspects of intellectual life.

- highly focused and probing deeply into the nature or essence of our world.

> ✳ Discovery consists of seeing what everybody has seen and thinking what nobody has thought.
>
> —ALBERT VON SZENT-GYORGYI

- sources of objective, well-thought-out advice.

- confident of their inspirations, ideas, and visions, regardless of popular beliefs.

- independent and not going along with the crowd.

- having a dry, understated wit.

- curious, open to well-thought-out ideas, and respectful of different opinions of those they see as competent.

What Others Find Challenging

People of other temperament types sometimes experience Knowledge Seekers as:

- acting superior and coming across as "know-it-alls."

> ✳ We should take care not to make the intellect our god; it has, of course, powerful muscles, but no personality.
> —ALBERT EINSTEIN

- not affectionate, sentimental, or generous with their time and resources. They can be seen as remote or detached, and make others feel as if they don't matter. They are sometimes hard to get close to and are emotionally unavailable.

- pedantic, argumentative, opinionated, and critical of other people's ideas and opinions, especially those whom they see as less competent or less intelligent than themselves.

- looking down on other people for being "too emotional."

- focused on goals rather than on people and their needs.

- brusque and intimidating. People can be afraid to stand up to them.

- abstract, cerebral, and difficult to understand.

Things Knowledge Seekers Would *Never* Dream of Doing

You'll never catch a Knowledge Seeker:

- missing an opportunity to hear a lecture at the university because they want to see their favorite soap opera.

- feeling totally refreshed after an evening of small talk.

- applying for a position as emcee for the Teen Miss America pageant.

- screaming and jumping up and down at a rock concert.

- commenting on sensitivity as a positive attribute.

- going to a new financial consultant or other "expert" without verifying their credentials.

How to Get Along with Knowledge Seekers

If you want to get along with Knowledge Seekers:

- Let them know you respect and appreciate their objectivity, competence, inventiveness, and ingenuity. Keep in mind that your praise must be specific to be credible.

- If you value the wisdom of their counsel, expertise, and advice, make sure you let them know. Also mention your appreciation of their intuitive insight.

- Respect their need for independence and autonomy. Develop your own interests and don't rely on them for all your companionship. Keep in mind that once they make a commitment, they usually like to be free to pursue their interests. It doesn't mean they don't care.

> ✳ Let there be spaces in your togetherness.
>
> —KAHLIL GIBRAN

- Don't pressure them to behave in socially acceptable ways. They may become passive, resistant, silent, or cold, and refuse to cooperate. Keep in mind that their autonomy is the basis of their self-respect.

- Don't expect effusive appreciation, lavish praise, or frequent reassurances of love and caring.

- Engage them in intellectually stimulating conversation. Debate or argue for fun or sport once in a while. They'll respect you for having and holding your view. Don't take their remarks personally, however.

- Value them for their objectivity, level-headeness, calm, and self-control.

- Try not to overwhelm them with your feelings. If you need to tell them that they offended or hurt you, do it calmly and precisely. Express your feelings without attacking or criticizing them. Remember, the Knowledge Seeker is highly self-critical already.

- If you want them to accept your suggestions, address the future implications of your ideas and show how they will fit into the big picture. Appeal to their sense of logic.

- If you offer them critical feedback about their ideas, be accurate and precise. They take constructive criticism as evidence that you have truly understood their ideas.

- Allow them to focus on the creative, more challenging aspects of a problem or project. Whenever possible, spare them the boredom of working out the details.

- When giving them an assignment, avoid giving confining directions. Knowledge Seekers may rebel and not bother to complete an assignment when they feel restricted by having to do things in a certain way.

- When they talk about their ideas, postpone addressing more realistic concerns or ruling out ideas that seem impractical. Don't nitpick about the details and specifics. Give them a chance to share the "big picture" with you.

- Avoid giving blow-by-blow descriptions of the details.

- Don't expect them to follow through on all of their ideas.

- Trust their ability to gather information through hunches and inspiration. Don't question them about why or how they "know."

- When they give you an assignment, ask them clarifying questions as to how to proceed. Don't panic if all the details are not immediately forthcoming, however. They may not know yet. Proceed on your own and seek more clarification later.

- Help them lighten up and get them out of their seriousness—when appropriate.

In addition to the comments above, the following suggestions can be particularly effective when dealing with Knowledge Seeker children:

- Provide them access to plenty of books, computer materials, building toys, and other creative projects.

- Encourage them to develop and master skills.

- Provide opportunities for them to be independent and self-sufficient.

- Don't fuss over them.

- Avoid confrontation by recognizing early signs of resistance. Say yes as often as you can. Save no for when it's imperative.

- When their behavior needs correcting, ask what they think would be a fair or reasonable solution.

- When asking them to do something, give them logical reasons for your request. Be patient with their inquisitiveness; Knowledge Seekers ask questions in order to understand things and are not necessarily trying to annoy you or to be contrary.

- Model open and honest communication of feelings. Teach by example the importance of gentleness, kindness, empathy, and sensitivity.

Practical Suggestions for Knowledge Seekers

RELATIONSHIPS

- When other people are talking about their personal problems, avoid analyzing and trying to "fix" them. Not every problem needs to be solved. Many times people just want to be heard and understood.

- Acknowledge others' accomplishments, even the little things they do. Show appreciation based on individual merit, not just on your standards.

> ❋ People are in greater need of your praise when they try
> and fail, than when they try and succeed.
> —BOB MOAWAD

- Learn to be more self-revealing about how you feel.

- Notice other people's interest or lack of interest in what you are talking about. Avoid talking over other people's heads. Focus on making an interpersonal connection, where you meet others on common ground, before proceeding with discussing your ideas.

> ❋ The chief merit of language is clearness, and we know
> that nothing detracts so much from this as do
> unfamiliar terms.
> —GALEN, 129–199

- Practice observing others' interactions with you. Notice the effect your behavior has on them. Become aware of people reacting defensively or withdrawing, as if they are intimidated by you. Respond with a gentle, open manner.

- Remember that what you see as hearty exchanges and debates may not be perceived that way by others.

- Be especially careful when you think someone is challenging your competency. Find out what the person really means before reacting or responding.

> ✳ A very popular error—having the courage of one's
> convictions: Rather it is a matter of having the courage for
> an attack upon one's convictions.
>
> —FRIEDRICH WILHELM NIETZSCHE

- Avoid taking others for granted. Take time to learn what matters to those you care about and to anticipate your loved ones' most important needs.

- When presenting a new idea, give people time to process and digest it.

- Engage other people's participation. People are quicker to accept changes and new ideas when they are invited to offer input and feedback.

PERSONAL GROWTH AND SELF-DEVELOPMENT

- Recognize the limits of rational thinking and cerebral understanding. Learn to access your heart and body, as well as your mind, for information.

> ✳ A good head and a good heart are always
> a formidable combination.
>
> —NELSON MANDELA

- Pay attention to physical clues in your body. They can help you identify your feelings.

- Beware of overworking and forgetting about your bodily needs. Engage in physical activity to channel stress through and out of your body. Try participatory sports, exercise, dancing, or yoga.

> ✳ To keep the body in good health is a duty...
> Otherwise we shall not be able to keep our mind strong
> and clear.
> —BUDDHA

- Expand your sense of self to include more than what you *do* or *produce*.

- Do things just for the fun of it, not to become more competent or to have more control.

> ✳ A person will be called to account on judgment day for
> every permissible thing that they might have enjoyed
> but did not.
> —JERUSALEM TALMUD

- Learn to recognize the simple joys of everyday life.

> ✳ Be glad of life because it gives you a chance to love and
> play and to look up at the stars.
> —HENRY VANDYKE

Famous Knowledge Seekers

- **Inventors and Scientists:** Stephen Hawking, Albert Einstein, Oliver Sacks, Linus Pauling, Thomas Edison, Marie Curie, Charles Darwin, Benjamin Franklin, Isaac Newton, Jonas Salk, Bill Gates

- **Writers and Philosophers:** Ayn Rand, Franz Kafka, Albert Camus, Krishnamurti, Edgar Allen Poe, James Joyce, Bill Moyers, Joseph Campbell, Timothy Leary, Carl Jung, Alan Watts, Immanuel Kant, René Descartes, Betty Friedan

- **Politicians/Presidents:** Theodore Roosevelt, Adlai Stevenson, Richard Nixon, Jerry Brown, Henry Kissinger, Ralph Nader, Hillary Clinton, Elizabeth Dole, Diane Feinstein, Alan Greenspan, Al Gore

- **Actors/Comedians/Entertainers/TV and Media Personalities:** David Letterman, Mort Sahl, George Carlin, Jay Leno, Woody Allen, Oscar Madison *(Odd Couple),* Katharine Hepburn, David Brinkley, Phil Donahue, Barbara Walters

- **Others Knowledge Seekers:** Frank Lloyd Wright, Napoleon, General Douglas MacArthur

6 *

Ideal Seekers

Approximately 10 percent of the U.S. population

To be nobody-but-yourself—
in a world which is doing its best,
night and day, to make you like everybody else—
means to fight the hardest battle
which any human being can fight;
and never stop fighting.

—E.E. CUMMINGS

Ideal Seekers are motivated by the need to discover and express their authentic selves, free of facades and pretenses. They search for personal meaning and significance in life. "Who am I?" is an ongoing question for them, and there's always a deeper level of meaning to explore.

Ideal Seekers are passionate about the things they believe in. They devote a great deal of time and energy to fostering and maintaining relationships, which they feel should be based on honesty, integrity, and genuineness. Ideal Seekers are keenly perceptive, insightful, and sensitive to feelings—their own and other people's. They are the most empathetic of all the temperaments. They want to help others realize their potential and achieve personal fulfillment. They place a high value on working toward an idealized and meaningful world where all individuals are self-actualized and contribute their gifts.

Relationships

In their relationships, Ideal Seekers:

- have a knack for knowing others' deeper motivations and for drawing out issues that need to be addressed.

- support others by trying to understand them more than by meeting their practical needs.

- are sensitive to the moods and feelings of others, especially when they are hurting or in conflict.

- seek a deep and meaningful relationship with an "ideal" partner who shares their values and goals.

- seek affirmation and approval from those important to them.

- value depth and authenticity in their relationships.

- prefer exploring a relationship deeply to see the potential for intimacy. Casual dating revolving around social events or activities is not usually appealing for very long.

- can sometimes be cautious about making a commitment, but when it feels right, commitment can bring them a sense of fulfillment and purpose.

- can be devoted mates, family members, and friends.

- are romantic and like giving gifts that have symbolic meaning (a special book, photo, poem, card).

- can project an idealized vision onto their lover, and can get caught up in the fantasy of the person rather than the reality.

- are willing to look at themselves and work on improving their relationships.

- try to promote harmonious relationships and can sometimes suppress their negative feelings, especially anger.

- invest a lot of effort, emotion, and enthusiasm in their relationships, sometimes more than people of other temperaments are comfortable with.

Ideal Seekers often do well in relationships with other Ideal Seekers because they can feel met in their strong need for deep connection, intimacy, and empathic communication.

Extroverted Ideal Seekers are verbally expressive and relate with warmth and affection to others. They can be charming and charismatic.

Introverted Ideal Seekers are more private about expressing their feelings, except with those close to them. They are deeply caring, but they can sometimes appear aloof, mysterious, or even indifferent.

Male Ideal Seekers sometimes have difficulty fitting in with mainstream American culture because they grow up being told that "real men" are tough-minded, independent, rational, objective, and unemotional. Their gentle, tender-hearted nature is often considered "unmasculine," "touchy feely," or even "wimpy," especially by other men, often including their fathers. Ideal Seekers often mask their nature to adapt and fit in. They sometimes compensate by being sexually seductive in an attempt to prove their manhood, or by developing their mental, intellectual side. Ideal Seeker men tend to relate more easily to women than men.

Female Ideal Seekers often have an easier time, because women are socialized to be more nurturing, sensitive, and compassionate.

Communication

Ideal Seekers like to ponder and discuss their fantasies, personal philosophy, spirituality, and matters of the heart. They are oriented more toward what is possible, or what might be, than toward what is actual or observable. They are not especially interested in talking about factual or concrete matters or the details and specifics of life (the weather, the stock market, finances, or the cost of living, for instance).

Ideal Seekers are highly sensitive to subtleties, nuances, and implications of communication—to a person's body language, facial expression, and vocal inflections. They are good at reading between the lines and perceiving underlying meanings. When communicating, they make intuitive leaps, moving quickly from the parts or the particulars to generalizations, patterns, and interconnections. Ideal Seekers trust their intuition and imagination.

Many Ideal Seekers have an ease with the spoken or written language. They imagine how their words and actions will affect others and want to be sensitive to their impact on others. Their language is often rich with metaphors and analogies, and they tend toward fanciful and imaginative speech—sometimes even poetry.

As Parents

As parents, Ideal Seekers:

- feel a strong sense of responsibility for their children's moral, spiritual, and emotional development and well-being.

- try to encourage their children's individuality and interests, and provide opportunities for their expression, even if very different from their own.

- seek to give their children respect and a voice in decisions, unless the child's viewpoint strongly conflicts with their own value system.

- are often accepting and tolerant and rarely impose unfeasible expectations on their children.

- are often patient and understanding listeners, and tolerant of a child's moods and feelings.

- try to promote harmonious relationships and are often the family peacekeeper.

- are often warm, gentle, and affectionate.

- want to have a close bond and rapport with their children and to be intimately involved in their lives into adulthood. It can be painful to them if their children are not interested in such a connection.

As Children and Teens

As children and teens, Ideal Seekers:

- often have rich and active imaginations and a wide range of interests and abilities. Many enjoy reading and participating in creative activities such as writing, acting, drawing, dance, and music.

- want to be valued and affirmed for being unique and are always looking to define their special place.

- are usually cooperative.

- flourish in a warm, loving, and harmonious atmosphere.

- respond well to praise and are hypersensitive to criticism. They can withdraw, become insecure, and lose confidence when criticized.

- have few defenses against negativity and conflict and can suffer tremendous emotional distress, or even physical illness, when they witness coldness or cruelty.

- are curious about new ideas and often do well academically. Their interests often span many subjects.

- do best competing against themselves. Competition with others can create division and disharmony.

- often try to emulate the best qualities of those they admire.

More than children of other temperaments, Ideal Seeker children can have trouble shrugging off expectations that don't fit them. If they don't feel understood, or if their inherent qualities are discouraged, punished, or not valued, they can hide their true nature and become lost to themselves. Some become rebellious, either secretly or overtly, in their teenage years.

Ideal Seeker children sometimes feel out of place or estranged from their classmates because there are so few of them in a classroom (only 10 percent, usually one or two in a class). This is true especially for *Introverted* Ideal Seekers who comprise only 1 percent of the population, until they go to college, where they find a higher percentage of kindred spirits. Elementary school teachers tend to be Security Seekers, so the classroom environment is generally set up by and for a different temperament type.

At Work

> ❇ How wonderful it is that nobody need wait a single moment before starting to improve the world.
> —ANNE FRANK, *DIARY OF A YOUNG GIRL*

At work, Ideal Seekers:

- like working with creative people.

- thrive in cooperative environments that reflect their values, where personal and professional growth and development are encouraged.

- like coming up with new and imaginative ways of doing things, and can motivate others with their creative ideas. They sometimes become bored with projects or tasks after the initial challenge wears off.

- can be inspirational and persuasive leaders in groups whose values are in accord with their own, especially *Extroverted* Ideal Seekers. The *Introverts* usually prefer to gently inspire and persuade from the background.

- are willing to work hard to achieve their ideals and long-range goals.

- often have a desire to be admired, respected, or to have fame. *Introverted* Ideal Seekers go about their quest in a more reserved, inconspicuous way than *Extroverts* do.

- are often determined to make a difference, especially in the lives of others. They can make significant and selfless contributions to the welfare of humankind.

- have a talent for diplomacy, bringing cooperation and unity.

- are often effective at conflict resolution and at building and maintaining morale.

- are effective in confronting individuals or groups about the impact of their behavior on relationships or group productivity.

- can be single-minded when defending their values and beliefs. This may not be obvious to others until these values are challenged or disregarded. Other people can sometimes be surprised by the strength of the Ideal Seeker's convictions.

> ✱ Happy is the man who ventures boldly to defend what he
> holds dear.
>
> —OVID

- can be too idealistic and independent-minded to work in traditional corporate, government, or military environments.

- are willing to follow policies and procedures, *if* they are compatible with their own values.

- can have an antiauthoritarian attitude and often side with the underdog.

- often have nonfinancial reasons for working (for self-expression, to uphold the values of a particular organization they believe in). Money tends not to be a priority. They are often not driven by conventional standards of external success.

Extroverted Ideal Seekers often like working collaboratively with creative people in active and stimulating environments. They can be inspiring and charismatic leaders and motivate others with their energy and enthusiasm.

Introverted Ideal Seekers often prefer working independently, behind the scenes. They go about their pursuits and tasks in a quiet, inconspicuous way. They can be highly focused, determined, and committed when their work is in line with their inner values. If they are willing to be visible, they can be persuasive and inspirational leaders.

Some Ideal Seekers are organized, orderly, decisive, and good at following through. They want to see their ideas developed and applied. Other Ideal Seekers are often enthusiastic about initiating projects but can have difficulty narrowing their focus and following through with things.

Careers

Many career paths are suitable for Ideal Seekers. The following is a list of some occupations that have proven to be satisfying for many because their strengths and abilities are being utilized.

- **Helping professions:** psychologist, psychotherapist, counselor, social worker, coach, mediator, clergy/ministry

- **Education:** teacher/professor (health, art, drama, English, special education, alternative education, music), resource development specialist, librarian, researcher, religious educator, interpreter/translator

- **Creative:** artist, designer, architect, graphic artist, photographer, actor, musician, composer, art director, editor, journalist, motivational speaker, writer (playwright, novelist, poet)

- **Health care:** occupational therapist, physician, nurse, physical therapist, dietitian/nutritionist, holistic health practitioner, speech pathologist, massage therapist, heath-care administrator

- **Business/Sales:** entrepreneur, marketer, business owner, executive (small business), restaurateur, consultant (beauty, hair, clothing, decorating)

- **Corporate/Professional:** corporate trainer, fund-raiser, organizational development consultant, public relations specialist, recruiter, conference planner, human resources development specialist, program designer, employee assistance program coordinator

Leisure

Ideal Seekers often enjoy reading and having meaningful discussions about psychology, spirituality, mysticism, philosophy, dreams, movies, books, relationships, and their purpose in life. Many like attending classes and workshops, and artistic and cultural events. Some like participating in community organizations and humanitarian causes. Most Ideal Seekers like having a balance between time alone for their many creative projects or activities and time with family and friends.

The more outgoing, *Extroverted* Ideal Seekers like having an active lifestyle and often have a wide circle of friends. Too much time alone sometimes causes them to become moody or bored.

The more reserved, *Introverted* Ideal Seekers like more time alone, for reading, reflection, and contemplating the mysteries of life. They usually prefer relating one-on-one or being with a small group of friends.

What's Hard About Being an Ideal Seeker

Ideal Seekers are stressed by:

- being overly sensitive to how they are seen by others.

> ✻ I was raised to sense what someone wanted me to be and be that kind of person. It took me a long time to not judge myself through someone else's eyes.
>
> —SALLY FIELD

- having high expectations of themselves and feeling guilty when they're not living up to their standards.

- not finding people who understand them and share their values and interests. They can feel a deep sense of emptiness and loss if they can't find and sustain empathic and meaningful relationships.

- not finding ways to realize their goals, and becoming discouraged, disillusioned, or disheartened.

- being in conflict between the need for connection and supporting others, and the need for solitude and taking care of themselves.

- feeling disappointed or neglected when they're not being appreciated or affirmed.

- not believing in or trusting themselves.

- becoming disillusioned or depressed when others don't see the need for peacefulness in the world.

- witnessing harshness, cruelty, or injustice, especially toward children.

> ✤ So long as little children are allowed to suffer, there is no true love in this world.
>
> —ISADORA DUNCAN

- becoming moody and obsessed with their intense inner world, and overcome by the dark side of life. This is especially true for *introverted* Ideal Seekers.

- never being quite certain of their sense of themselves.

- persevering through the more mundane routines of life.

- failing to set limits and boundaries and being taken advantage of by others.

Peeves

Superficial relationships

Insincerity

Meaningless chatter

Sarcasm and teasing

Hostile or competitive environments

Tension and conflict

Too much routine

Too many rules or policies

Valuing expediency over integrity

People who are emotionally unresponsive or cold

What Others Admire

People of other temperament often experience Ideal Seekers as:

- warm-hearted, personable, genuine, empathetic, and compassionate, offering others a sense of unconditional love.

> ❀ She did not talk to people as if they were strong hard shells she had to crack open to get inside. She talked as if she were already in the shell. In their very shell.
>
> —MARITA BONNER

- generous in expressing heartfelt appreciation and approval of others.

- perceptive, insightful, and wise.

- knowing how to draw people out and gain insight into their values and life purpose.

- seeing the potential good in people and humanity.

- curious, open to new ideas, and respectful of different opinions, unless they strongly conflict with the Ideal Seekers' deeper values.

- interesting to talk to and often good listeners.

> ✽ The most called-upon prerequisite of a friend is an accessible ear.
>
> —MAYA ANGELOU

- graceful in handling situations and people tactfully and diplomatically.

- original and creative in their contributions.

- passionate about the things they believe in, and effective in sharing their enthusiasm with others.

- morally principled, and able to inspire and influence people toward higher values and goals.

What Others Find Challenging

People of other temperaments sometimes view Ideal Seekers as:

- overly sensitive, easily offended, and prone to attribute unintended meaning to communications or actions.

- overly focused on their ideals and sometimes impractical and unrealistic.

> ❀ Idealism is fine, but as it approaches reality the cost
> becomes prohibitive.
> —WILLIAM F. BUCKLEY, JR.

- self-righteous and stubborn when they believe their core values have been violated.

- giving too much credence to their feelings.

- self-absorbed in their search for meaning. Their complex personalities are often puzzling to others, even to themselves.

- not accepting others as fallible human beings, who may not live up to their fantasies or ideals.

- neglecting their loved ones by becoming overly involved in their projects or causes.

- placing too much emphasis on love or romance and being too eager to seek intimacy.

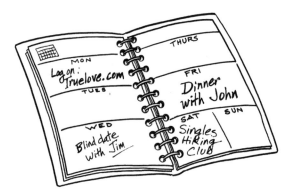

Things Ideal Seekers Would *Never* Dream of Doing

You'll never catch an Ideal Seeker:

- telling a friend they have no time to listen to them and not giving any reasons why.

- taking a job in the Housing Eviction Department.

- lobbying against the Clean Air Bill.

- signing the petition to continue deforestation in the lumber industry.

- teaching a course in How to Get Ahead in the World by Stepping on People's Toes.

How to Get Along with Ideal Seekers

If you want to get along with Ideal Seekers:

- Let them know you value and appreciate their warmth, compassion, genuineness, perceptiveness, insightfulness, and creativity.

- Take the time to really listen to them—to their feelings, values, dreams, and aspirations.

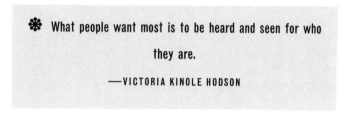

❀ What people want most is to be heard and seen for who they are.

—VICTORIA KINOLE HODSON

- Engage them in open dialogue and personal sharing.

- Be willing to work things out in the face of conflict.

- Don't judge them for their changing moods.

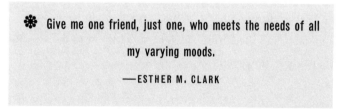

❀ Give me one friend, just one, who meets the needs of all my varying moods.

—ESTHER M. CLARK

- Be understanding and patient about their need to process and express their feelings. Avoid discounting, dismissing, or making light of their feelings, even if you think they have no rational or logical basis.

- Encourage them to follow their personal and creative pursuits and to put their work out in the world.

- Reassure them that you will not reject them or be angry with them if they set a boundary and say no when asked to do something.

- Be very tactful when offering feedback. Ideal Seekers are highly sensitive to disapproval, rejection, and criticism.

> ❉ There are worse words than cuss words, there are words
> that hurt.
>
> —TILLIE OLSEN

- Avoid being competitive or combative.

- Give them freedom and autonomy. Even though they can encourage dependence in others, they can become irritated if people become clingy, needy, or demanding of their attention.

- Don't give them all the details of your day. Learn to share the highlights.

- When they talk about their ideas, refrain from automatically ruling out those that seem unrealistic or impractical. Help them figure out ways of implementing their ideas. Don't expect them to follow thorough on all their ideas, however.

> ❀ The best way to have a good idea is to have
>
> lots of ideas.
>
> —LINUS PAULING

In addition to the above suggestions, the following might be helpful for relating to Ideal Seeker children:

- Be gentle when you correct misbehavior. Apologize quickly and sincerely if you lose your temper or raise your voice.

- Try to foster a supportive environment.

- Honor their individual uniqueness. Don't squelch their imagination, enthusiasm, or creativity.

- Remind them they are loved for who they are, not for what they do.

- Provide them with a variety of creative outlets. Encourage them to try out many hobbies and creative outlets without expecting them to make a long commitment to any one of them.

Practical Suggestions for Ideal Seekers

SELF-ACCEPTANCE/SELF-NURTURING

- Honor your values and make choices based on them—even if it seems that the rest of the world does not understand.

> ❀ Let me listen to me and not to them.
>
> —GERTRUDE STEIN

- Practice accepting some things as they are rather than trying to make everything over according to your ideal vision.

- Respect your need for time to dream, fantasize, read, and create.

> ❋ So you see, imagination needs moodling—
> long, inefficient, happy idling, dawdling, and uttering.
> —BRENDA UELAND

- Learn to accept both sides of your nature, your anger as well as your benevolent feelings.

- Avoid overdosing on self-analysis and giving too much credence to your feelings. Express your feelings through writing, art, or talking, and then move on.

- See your moods as transitory. Know that they will change.

- Learn to enjoy the here and now, and the everyday realities of life.

RELATIONSHIPS

- Beware of excessive responsiveness to other people's needs. Communicate your limits and boundaries to others.

- Avoid taking every comment and remark personally. Learn to be more objective and to discern what is actually being communicated, not just what is "between the lines."

- Realize that rejection of your ideas is not a rejection of you.

• Be realistic about how much acceptance you can reasonably expect from others. Learn to evaluate your worth without depending on other people's views. Try to be less dependent on external affirmation. Look for internal affirmation instead.

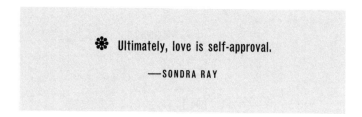

❋ Ultimately, love is self-approval.

—SONDRA RAY

• When meeting someone new, ask practical questions before leaping into a relationship. Avoid projecting positive qualities on others that are not really there.

- Be aware of finding fault with others when they don't meet your ideals. Remember that others are only human and have a mix of good and bad qualities.

- Seek out friends who understand and appreciate you and encourage you to be yourself.

> ❋ Home is not where you live but where
> they understand you.
> —CHRISTIAN MORGENSTERN

- Go to places where other Ideal Seekers are likely to be, such as classes in psychology, literature, art, metaphysics, and spirituality, poetry readings, and human potential workshops.

- When conflicts arise, try to be direct and to express yourself honestly, rather than silently withdrawing as a way to set limits.

- Avoid trying to help people who have not asked for help. Try to be aware of when it's appropriate to give someone a push and when it's not.

WORK

- Set realistic goals so you won't feel disappointed if you don't accomplish all you had hoped. Let go of unrealistic expectations of yourself. Learn to appreciate and acknowledge your present level of success and achievement.

- Look for work that fits your ideals and interests. Make sure it allows you to be an individual and to express yourself.

- Avoid choosing careers to please others, particularly careers that might be easy for you to pursue but difficult to cope with emotionally such as engineering, accounting, and science.

Famous Ideal Seekers

- **Crusaders/Spiritual Leaders**: Mahatma Gandhi, Nelson Mandela, Martin Luther King, Jr., Don Quixote, Joan of Arc, Susan B. Anthony, Eleanor Roosevelt

- **Actors/Entertainers**: Audrey Hepburn, Oprah Winfrey, Marlo Thomas, Jane Fonda, Robin Williams, Whoopie Goldberg, Dustin Hoffman, Danny Glover

- **Directors**: Ingmar Bergman, Steven Spielberg

- **Musicians**: Joan Baez, Joni Mitchell, Judy Collins, Paul Simon, Art Garfunkel

- **Writers**: Emily Dickinson, Danielle Steele, Zelda Fitzgerald, Simone de Beauvoir, Alice Walker, Toni Morrison, Maya Angelou, Annie Lamott

- **Politicians**: Jimmy Carter, Bill Clinton

- **Psychologists**: Carl Rogers, Abraham Maslow, Sigmund Freud, Wayne Dyer

- **Other Famous Ideal Seekers**: Jacqueline Kennedy, Yoko Ono, Prince Charles

Final Thoughts

*

Although temperaments do not explain everything about people, they certainly give us a great deal of practical insight into human behavior, which can have a life-transforming effect on our relationships with ourselves and others.

For those of you who were not allowed or encouraged to be your true selves when growing up, I hope the information helps you to undo the negative messages you received in childhood, and to realize that it's all right to be the kind of person you are. If you are not already doing so, I hope this information encourages you to develop your natural strengths and abilities and to pursue the work that you are best suited for. I hope this understanding helps you to accept, respect, and validate your own and other peoples' strengths and abilities, and brings greater harmony and peace in your relationships with others.

I am grateful to have had the opportunity to share this valuable information, which has changed my own life in profound ways. Twenty years ago, when I learned about temperament, it started me on my path of self-acceptance and helped me to realize that it was all right to be me. I hope it has an equally powerful effect on you.

Appendix

Correlating the Temperaments with the Enneagram

Readers who identify with temperament types might find it useful to learn about other personality systems. One such system, the Enneagram, is particularly descriptive, and meshes well with temperament theory.

The Enneagram

The Enneagram is a system of nine personality types whose roots go back many centuries. The word *Enneagram* (pronounced "ANY-a-gram") comes from the Greek words *ennea*, which means "nine," and *gram*, which means "map" or "drawing." No one knows the exact origins of the Enneagram, but it is said to date back several thousand years. The Enneagram was taught orally in secret Sufi brotherhoods in the Middle East, and the Russian mystic and spiritual teacher Gurdjieff introduced it to Europe in the 1920s. It arrived in South America in the late 1960s through Oscar Ichazo and his Arica Institute in Chile. Ichazo's student Claudio Naranjo brought the Enneagram to the United States, where it was enthusiastically embraced and expounded by Jesuit priests and the psychological community.

The Enneagram is represented by a circle that surrounds a nine-pointed star, whose points are each labeled with a different personality type. The nine types are divided into three triads, according to the center of intelligence—the heart or feeling, head or thinking, and gut or instinctual. The triads express the three different ways people experience or know the world. Even though we all come into the world with a capacity for feeling, thinking, and instincts, we become most identified with one of these centers. One of the goals of working with the Enneagram is to bring all three centers of intelligence into balance. As we will see, the centers loosely correlate to the temperaments, and combine with them in interesting ways. Although there are no exact correlations between them, you will see that some temperaments are very common for certain Enneagram centers and types. For instance, in the thinking center, the analytical and objective Enneagram type Fives are very often Knowledge Seekers. In the Feeling center, the warm and compassionate Enneagram type Fours are often Ideal Seekers (and rarely any other temperament).

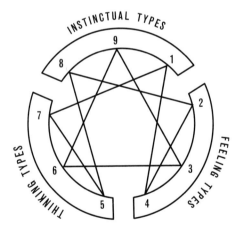

Unlike temperaments, which to a large extent we are born with, our Enneagram type represents the ways in which we have adapted ourselves to function within our family and society. In our attempt to gain love and approval, we developed a coping strategy based on our natural strengths and abilities. Thus, our strategy became our defensive structure, which was further impacted by the expectations and demands of our parents and other caregivers. While our survival strategy made us feel relatively safe and secure, it also limited our perceptions, thoughts, and actions. Our Enneagram type is a way of describing how we think, perceive, and respond to life.

Although we have some traits in common with all the types, the underlying motivation of each type is different. As you read the description of the Enneagram types you may relate to some of the qualities of the various types, but keep in mind that each person has only one core type that represents his or her basic personality.

If you would like to learn more about the Enneagram, I suggest you read my introductory book, *The Enneagram Made Easy*, cowritten with Elizabeth Wagele (see Resources section).

Here is a brief description of the Nine Enneagram types. For each type you will find a listing for the four temperaments (Security Seekers, Experience Seekers, Knowledge Seekers, and Ideal Seekers) as they relate to that type.

FEELING TYPES:

Two: Helpers are motivated by the need to be loved, appreciated, and needed. Twos take pride in their ability to make people feel special by anticipating and fulfilling their needs. Helping, understanding, and making others feel valued gives Twos the approval and acknowledgment they need to feel wanted and loved. They almost always take better care of others than they do of themselves. Twos appear cheerful, self-sufficient, and confident and they avoid appearing needy. They are dependent on others for approval, reassurance, recognition, and a sense of self-worth.

On the positive side, Twos are warm, generous, empathic, nurturing, and supportive. They relate easily to people, enjoy giving to others, and are capable of unconditional love. On the negative side, they can be manipulative (giving to get), clingy, possessive, and martyrlike. When people don't appreciate their giving, they can become disappointed, hurt, or demanding. After keeping mental score of all they've given, Twos can feel entitled to be taken care of by others.

SECURITY SEEKER TWOS

Responsible, dependable, loyal, and devoted. Show love in practical ways by doing things for others. Value harmony and traditions. Concerned with being socially appropriate. Most often warm-hearted, friendly, feeling types.

EXPERIENCE SEEKER TWOS

Enthusiastic, energetic, friendly, and fun-loving. Generous and helpful in practical ways. Most often caring and compassionate. Feeling types.

KNOWLEDGE SEEKER TWOS

This is an uncommon type. The objective, logical, analytical, and emotionally detached qualities of Knowledge Seekers are not often found in the Helper personality.

IDEAL SEEKER TWOS

Warm-hearted, nurturing, supportive, empathetic, and compassionate. Perceptive and insightful. Full of enthusiasm and new ideas. Persuasive, inspiring, and expressive. Good communicators. Often outgoing and extroverted.

Three: Achievers are motivated by the need to be productive, efficient, and successful at whatever they do. Admiration and praise for being a "winner" gives them self-esteem and makes them feel worthwhile. For Threes, life is a series of tasks to be completed and goals to be reached, and they keep pushing themselves to achieve more. When they're not achieving or measuring up to the standards they've set for themselves, they can feel inadequate. In order to get things done, Threes avoid introspection and self-reflection and ignore the guidance from their own feelings. Threes identify with the roles they play and they can alter, change, or modify their image to mirror others' expectations of them. To impress and gain approval, Threes can end up deceiving themselves and others by presenting a false public persona, representing themselves as more or different than they really are.

On the positive side, Threes are energetic, optimistic, confident, self-assured, and competent. They often make good leaders who motivate others to live up to their potential. On the negative side, Threes can be vain, overly competitive, deceitful, narcissistic, and opportunistic.

SECURITY SEEKER THREES

Conscientious, hard-working, and responsible. Realistic, practical, pragmatic, and efficient. Determined and decisive. Goal-oriented. Confident and competent. Enjoy administrating and being in charge. More often extroverted, thinking types.

EXPERIENCE SEEKER THREES

Realistic, practical, pragmatic, and efficient. Like risk and challenge. Respond well to crisis. Energetic and constantly on the go. Confident, competent, and resourceful. Direct and straightforward. More often extroverted, thinking types.

KNOWLEDGE SEEKER THREES

Innovative, enterprising, and resourceful in solving challenging problems, especially theoretical ones. Confident and competent. Often leaders. Logical, analytical, and objective. Outspoken, straightforward, and direct.

IDEAL SEEKER THREES

Helpful, supportive, and empathetic. Value harmony and cooperation. Energetic, enthusiastic, and expressive. Good at motivating, inspiring, and persuading others. Ambitious and goal-oriented. Enjoy leadership positions. Often outgoing, extroverted types.

Four: Romantics are motivated by the need to understand and express their deepest feelings and to discover what is authentic in themselves. Fours want to feel unique and special, and they avoid being seen as ordinary. They have a keen sense of aesthetics and often express themselves symbolically through their art or creativity. Fours' attention is focused on what is missing, distant, and idealized, and they have difficulty enjoying being in the present, where few things are ever truly "ideal." Fours yearn for deep emotional connection to make them feel whole and complete. When they achieve a relationship, however, it often loses its value, which continues the cycle of longing for the unattainable or idealized.

On the positive side, Fours are imaginative, intuitive, creative, and compassionate. Introspective and self-aware, they are in touch with the hidden depths of human nature. On the negative side, Fours can be self-absorbed, hypersensitive, impractical, self-loathing, moody, and depressed. They are envious of those who seem more fulfilled, accomplished, or successful.

SECURITY SEEKER FOURS

This is not a common type. The practical, down-to-earth, realistic, dutiful, conservative, and traditional qualities of Security Seekers are unlike the Four personality type. The few exceptions tend to introverted, feeling types.

EXPERIENCE SEEKER FOURS

Experience Seeker Fours are rare. The few exceptions tend to be gentle, easygoing, adaptable, and compassionate. Often introverted, feeling types.

KNOWLEDGE SEEKER FOURS

Knowledge Seeker Fours are not common. Their objective, analytical, and emotionally detached qualities are unlike the Four personality type. The few exceptions tend to be introspective and introverted. They are more relationship-oriented, tuned in, and sensitive to people.

IDEAL SEEKER FOURS

Deep, intense, and complex. Have passionate convictions. Creative, imaginative, and individualistic. Insightful and perceptive. Sensitive, empathic, and compassionate. Seek to discover their authentic selves. Ideal Seeker Fours, especially introverted types, are quite common.

THINKING TYPES:

Five: Observers are motivated by the need to be knowledgeable, competent, independent, and self-sufficient. They avoid feeling or being dependent, vulnerable, incapable, or incompetent. Fives value logic, objectivity, and reason. Thinking and analyzing enables them to stay in their head and not be overwhelmed by their emotions. Intellectualizing helps them feel safer and makes life more controllable. Fives feel the need to carefully guard their time and energy and to keep everyone at a safe distance. They can easily feel invaded, overwhelmed, intruded upon, and drained by the needs or demands of others. Fives often want to find a niche, or an area of expertise that no one else has discovered where they can excel.

On the positive side, Fives are objective, level-headed, calm, insightful, ingenious, and curious. They are acutely observant of everything around them. On the down or negative side, they can be intellectually arrogant, withholding, controlled, cynical, negative, standoffish, and stingy.

SECURITY SEEKER FIVES

Realistic, practical, and matter-of-fact. Dependable, reliable, purposeful, and persevering. Organized, orderly, systematic, and precise. Concentrate well. Focused on facts. Reserved, quiet, and self-contained. Often introverted, thinking types.

EXPERIENCE SEEKER FIVES

Realistic, practical, and pragmatic. Enjoy working with tools and machines. Technically oriented. Independent, detached, and reserved. Often introverted, thinking types. Feeling type Experience Seekers are uncommon.

KNOWLEDGE SEEKER FIVES

Logical, analytical, and theoretical. Innovative and ingenious problem solvers. Have great insight and vision. Scholarly. Value precision in thought and language. Objective, impersonal, and detached. Independent and autonomous. Knowledge Seeker Fives, especially introverted types, are quite common.

IDEAL SEEKERS FIVES

This type is not common. The few exceptions tend to be quite tuned-in and sensitive to others. Absorbed in their creative projects. Introspective and reserved. Often introverted.

Six: Questioners are motivated by the need for security, safety, and predictability. They often look to some person, group, or cause to identify with and depend upon. Sixes are often suspicious of authority and uncomfortable being the authority. Sixes scan for danger and potential threat and anticipate where fear might arise. They have an active imagination when it comes to what might be threatening their safety and security. Most Sixes are either phobic or counterphobic and can appear entirely different from one another since they have the opposite reaction to fear. Phobic Sixes are timid and cautious, avoiding danger and potential attack. Counterphobic Sixes can act tough in an outspoken, challenging, and aggressive manner and are compelled to meet danger head-on. Many Sixes vacillate between phobic and counterphobic behavior.

On the positive side, Sixes are trustworthy, responsible, intellectually astute, and have an offbeat sense of humor. They value loyalty to family, friends, groups, and causes, and are often compassionate and sympathetic to the underdog. On the negative side, they can be hypervigilant, indecisive, defensive, self-defeating, paranoid, distrustful, doubtful about the people and events around them, and preoccupied with worst-case scenarios.

SECURITY SEEKER SIXES

Dependable, loyal, and trustworthy. Responsible, conscientious, and hard-working. Value consistency and stability. Honor and respect the customs, traditions, and social standards of society. Seek to belong. Often cautious, phobic types.

EXPERIENCE SEEKER SIXES

Spontaneous and impulsive. Realistic, practical, and pragmatic. Action-oriented. Like challenge. Often risk-takers who do well in a crisis. Value fraternal, egalitarian relationships. More often antiauthoritarian, counterphobic, thinking types.

KNOWLEDGE SEEKER SIXES

Logical, analytical, and theoretical. Innovative and ingenious problem solvers. Have great insight and vision. Independent and autonomous. Thrive on challenge and debate. Often antiauthoritarian, counterphobic types.

IDEAL SEEKER SIXES

Caring, concerned, supportive, and compassionate. Dependable, loyal, and trustworthy. Conscientious and responsible. Demanding of themselves. Value personal integrity. Often motivated by underdog causes.

Seven: Adventurers are motivated by the need to be happy and to keep anxiety at bay by staying busy and having lots of options and plans for new experiences. Sevens avoid boredom, suffering, painful emotions, and the everyday drudgeries of life as much as possible, deflecting them with optimism, humor, and positive thinking. They approach life with exuberance and enthusiasm, and put a lot of energy into the things that interest them. Sevens are constant seekers of excitement. They view life as a fun-filled adventure, yet they also want to contribute to the world. Sevens feel entitled to the good life and do not want to feel deprived.

On the positive side, Sevens are optimistic, enthusiastic, energetic, idealistic, generous, and often multitalented. They uplift and enliven others and are often fun to be around. On the negative side, they can be self-centered, self-indulgent, narcissistic, and hyperactive. They can be scattered and undisciplined and have problems with long-term commitment and follow-through.

SECURITY SEEKER SEVENS

This type is not common. The exceptions tend to be more practical, grounded, and down-to-earth. Less prone to be impulsive risk-takers. Organized, decisive, and good at follow-through. More often outgoing, extroverted types.

EXPERIENCE SEEKER SEVENS

Like variety, excitement, freedom, and independence. Realistic and pragmatic. Action-oriented. Respond well to crisis. Optimistic, enthusiastic, energetic, and fun-loving. Little tolerance for routine. Difficulty with completion and follow-through. Experience Seeker Sevens, especially extroverted types, are quite common.

KNOWLEDGE SEEKER SEVENS

Innovative, ingenious, and enterprising. Resourceful in solving challenging problems, especially theoretical ones. Value freedom and independence.

Thrive on challenge and debate. Resistant to being limited or controlled. Question authority. Persuasive, confident, and outspoken. Often extroverted.

IDEAL SEEKER SEVENS

Imaginative, creative, and full of new ideas. Often multitalented. Helpful, supportive, and compassionate. Value freedom and autonomy. Dislike routine. Good communicators. Insightful and perceptive. Persuasive and inspiring. Enthusiastic, energetic, and dynamic. Often extroverted.

INSTINCTUAL TYPES:

Eight: Asserters are motivated by the need to feel powerful, self-reliant, and to have control over their lives. They avoid being weak, vulnerable, controlled, or taken advantage of. Eights often have a forceful and formidable presence. They are often natural leaders who want to make an impact on the world. Being respected for their strength is more important to them than being liked. Eights have persistence and tenacity in going after what they want. Eights like the excitement of a righteous struggle for truth and justice and are willing to protect the underdog. They are often earthy and lusty, and seek intensity in all manners of stimulation.

On the positive side, Eights are dynamic, confident, direct, decisive, and dependable. They are courageous and protective of their loved ones and those who need defending. On the negative side, they can be aggressive, confrontive, domineering, self-centered, insensitive, and prone to excess.

SECURITY SEEKER EIGHTS

Responsible, hard-working, and goal-oriented. Practical, pragmatic, and down-to-earth. Organized, efficient, and decisive. Like responsibility, control, and being in charge. Meet challenges head-on. Assertive, direct, and outspoken. Argumentative and opinionated. Often extroverted, thinking types.

EXPERIENCE SEEKER EIGHTS

Spontaneous and impulsive. Energetic and gregarious. Have a zest for life. Value freedom and independence. Realistic, pragmatic, and practical. Have common sense. Outspoken and direct. Often antiauthoritarian, thinking types.

KNOWLEDGE SEEKER EIGHTS

Independent and autonomous. Dynamic, confident, and powerful. Enterprising and resourceful. Analytical and theoretical. Often take charge and mobilize resources to achieve long-range goals. Determined, driven, and goal-oriented. Direct, outspoken, confrontive, and challenging.

IDEAL SEEKER EIGHTS

This type is not common. The exceptions tend to be warm-hearted, nurturing, supportive, and compassionate. Less controlling unless pushed or treated unfairly. Empowering and protective of the underdog or those under their care.

Nine: Peacemakers are motivated by the need to maintain their inner stability, peace of mind, and tranquillity. They prefer a predictable, comfortable, harmonious life. Nines like to merge with others and with their environment, and they gain their sense of self through these connections. They tend to forget their own needs and priorities in order to accommodate others and to avoid conflict. They are often more aware of other people's agendas and priorities than their own. Nines can be disconnected from their own emotions, especially anger and resentment. They can become distracted from their priorities and divert their attention to trivial tasks, and procrastinate doing the things they need to do.

On the positive side, Nines are adaptable, easygoing, good-natured, supportive, compassionate, patient, and nonjudgmental. They see all sides of an issue and often make good mediators. On the negative side, they can be indecisive, spaced-out, distracted, apathetic, undisciplined, and unassertive.

Their anger can come out indirectly in stubbornness, inactivity, and passive-aggressiveness.

SECURITY SEEKER NINES

Dependable, loyal, and trustworthy. Averse to conflict. Conservative and traditional. Gentle, modest, unassuming, and reserved. More often introverted, feeling types.

EXPERIENCE SEEKER NINES

Easygoing and adaptable. Have a "live and let live" attitude. Appreciate the simple things in life. Accommodating, agreeable, accepting, and nonjudmental. Value harmony. Sensitive to conflict. Reserved, modest, and unassuming. Gentle and compassionate. Often introverted, feeling types.

KNOWLEDGE SEEKER NINES

This type is uncommon. The exceptions tend to be analytical and objective. Independent and strong-willed. Prefer doing things their own way. Resistant to being manipulated or controlled. More often reserved, introverted types.

IDEAL SEEKER NINES

Gentle, calm, easygoing, and adaptable. Committed and devoted to what they believe. Empathetic and compassionate. Value harmony. Cooperative and agreeable unless crossed. Contemplative and reserved. More often introverted.

One: Perfectionists are motivated by the need to live the right way. This includes improving themselves, others, and the world around them. Ones seek perfection in areas where they believe that they have the ideal vision of what "should be" (social reform, career goals, and what they perceive as proper manners, to name a few). Ones have a strong inner critic that requires them to live by a set of strict internal rules and unrealistically high standards. Being perfect and in control helps keep their inner critic at bay.

Ones drive themselves to do what they believe they "should" do, suppressing their natural impulses and desires in the process.

On the positive side, Ones are self-disciplined, hard-working, realistic, organized, and productive. They have integrity, high principles, and ideals. On the negative side, Ones can be rigid, inflexible, controlling, self-righteous, and hypercritical of themselves and others. Ones vent their resentment indirectly in the form of judgment, "helpful" criticism, sarcasm, "righteous" anger, or through an attitude of moral superiority.

SECURITY SEEKER ONES

Conscientious, responsible, practical, and hard-working. Dependable and trustworthy. Organized, orderly, practical, and precise. Traditional and conservative. Tend toward black-and-white thinking. Do what is "right" and expect the same of others.

EXPERIENCE SEEKER ONES

This type is not common. The exceptions tend to be practical, pragmatic, action-oriented, and less rule bound. More often introverted, antiauthoritarian, thinking types.

KNOWLEDGE SEEKER ONES

Analytical and objective. Resourceful in solving complex problems. Organized, determined, and decisive. Have strong convictions and principles. Drive themselves and others toward goals and self-improvement. Independent, strong willed, and self-determined. Often in charge.

IDEAL SEEKER ONES

Conscientious, responsible, and trustworthy. Empathic and compassionate. Single-minded regarding personal values and convictions and committed to their inspirations and ideals. Good at motivating and persuading others. Value self-improvement. Demanding of themselves.

Resources

TEMPERAMENT AND TYPE BOOKS

Baron, Renee. *What Type Am I?* New York: Penguin, 1998.

Kiersey, David. *Please Understand Me II.* Del Mar, Calif.: Prometheus Nemesis Books, 1998.

Kroeger, Otto, and Janet Thuesen. *Type Talk.* New York: Delacorte Press, 1988

———. *Type Talk at Work: How the 16 Types Determine Your Success on the Job.* New York: Delacorte Press, 1992.

Myers, Isabel Briggs, with Peter B. Myers. *Gifts Differing.* Palo Alto, Calif.: Consulting Psychologists Press, 1995.

Tieger, Paul, and Barbara Barron-Tieger. *Do What You Are.* Boston: Little, Brown, 1992.

———. *Nurture by Nature.* Boston: Little, Brown, 1997.

———. *Just Your Type.* Boston: Little, Brown, 2000.

BOOKLETS

Berens, Linda. *Understanding Yourself and Others.* Huntington Beach, Calif.: Telos, 2000

Berens, Linda, and Dario Nardi. *The 16 Sixteen Personality Types.* Huntington Beach, Calif.: Telos, 1999

ENNEAGRAM BOOKS

Baron, Renee, and Elizabeth Wagele. *The Enneagram Made Easy.* San Francisco: Harper, 1994.

——. *Are You My Type, Am I Yours?* San Francisco: Harper, 1995.

Riso, Don Richard and Russ Hudson. *The Wisdom of the Enneagram.* New York: Bantam Book, 1999.

OTHER RESOURCES

The Temperament Research Institute
16152 Beach Boulevard Suite 179
Huntington Beach, CA 92647

Association for Psychological Type (APT)
9140 Ward Parkway
Kansas City, MO 64114

Center for Applications of Psychological Type (CAPT)
2720 N.W. 6th Street
Gainesville, FL 32609

Consulting Psychologists Press, Inc. (CPP)
3803 East Bayshore Road
Palo Alto, CA 94303

Otto Kroeger Associates
Fairfax Crossroads
3605-C Chain Bridge Road
Fairfax, VA 22030

Type Resources, Inc.
101 Chestnut Street, H-135
Gaithersburg, MD 20877

The Temperament Research Institute
16152 Beach Boulevard Suite 179
Huntington Beach, CA 92647

About the Author

Renee Baron's twenty-five years of professional experience includes work with self-esteem enhancement, parent effectiveness, dream work, career counseling, recovery work, and Enneagram and Myers-Briggs personality assessments. She is available for counseling in person or by telephone.

To contact Renee:

e-mail: reneebaron@aol.com

Internet: www.reneebaron.com